SHALOM AND THE COMMUNITY OF CREATION

PROPHETIC CHRISTIANITY

Series Editors

Bruce Ellis Benson
Malinda Elizabeth Berry
Peter Goodwin Heltzel

The Prophetic Christianity series explores the complex relationship between Christian doctrine and contemporary life. Deeply rooted in the Christian tradition yet taking postmodern and postcolonial perspectives seriously, series authors navigate difference and dialogue constructively about divisive and urgent issues of the early twenty-first century. The books in the series are sensitive to historical contexts, marked by philosophical precision, and relevant to contemporary problems. Embracing shalom justice, series authors seek to bear witness to God's gracious activity of building beloved community.

God dwells in His creation and is everywhere indivisibly present in all His works. This is boldly taught by prophet and apostle and is accepted by Christian theology generally. That is, it appears in the books but for some reason it has not sunk into the average Christian's heart so as to become a part of his believing self. Christian teachers shy away from its full implications, and, if they mention it at all, mute it down until it has little meaning.

A. W. Tozer, *The Pursuit of God*

Long before I ever heard of Christ, or saw a White man, I had learned from an untutored woman the essence of morality. With the help of dear Nature herself, she taught me things simple but of mighty import. I knew God. I perceived what goodness is. I saw and I loved what is really beautiful. Civilization has not taught me anything better!

Charles Eastman (Dakota Indian)

Shalom and the Community of Creation

An Indigenous Vision

Randy S. Woodley

2012

WILLIAM B. EERDMANS PUBLISHING COMPANY
GRAND RAPIDS, MICHIGAN / CAMBRIDGE, U.K.

Published 2012 by
Wm. B. Eerdmans Publishing Co.
2140 Oak Industrial Drive N.E., Grand Rapids, Michigan 49505 /
P.O. Box 163, Cambridge CB3 9PU U.K.
www.eerdmans.com

Printed in the United States of America

17 16 15 14 13 12   7 6 5 4 3 2 1

Library of Congress Cataloging-in-Publication Data

Woodley, Randy, 1956-
Shalom and the community of creation: an indigenous vision / Randy S. Woodley.
        p.   cm.   — (Prophetic Christianity)
Includes bibliographical references (p.   ).
ISBN 978-0-8028-6678-3 (pbk.: alk. paper)
1. Creation.   2. God (Christianity) — Omnipresence.
3. Indians of North America — Religion.   I. Title.

BS651.W725   2012
230.089′97 — dc23
                                                2012009875

To the people who went before me and showed me the way of creation, especially my mother and the love she always showed for God's special world of animals, birds, and plants. You showed me how all things have life.

For my children and the next seven generations —
may you always remember our ways.

Contents

Foreword

Sitting in the bleachers of a Seattle-area high school gymnasium, I listened intently to the words of my friends, Randy and Edith Woodley. I was visiting the Pacific Northwest for a speaking engagement, and Randy and his family graciously agreed to accompany me to my very first powwow. I tried not to ask too many questions as Randy patiently narrated the powwow unfolding before us. I sat enthralled at the richness of the culture being revealed on the gym floor. The visual display was only a part of the learning experience for me. More importantly, I delighted in the privilege of hearing my friend weave vivid explication, cultural insight, theological wisdom, and truthtelling into a compelling narrative. As an outsider to the community, I was honored that the Woodleys would extend such authentic hospitality toward me. Later, I did what any twenty-first-century American would do — I Facebooked my experience: "Went to my first powwow with Randy and Edith Woodley. Everyone should have this experience."

American Christians are increasingly aware of the diversity that comprises Christianity in America. Multiethnic, multiracial, and multicultural ministry (we often use these three terms interchangeably, oftentimes incorrectly, conflating the three terms) is now in vogue. Diversity is applied superficially. Usually the application of multiculturalism (or any of the other terms) degenerates into tokenism. Churches and Christian organizations look for diversity in how we appear to outsiders. Diversity looks particularly nice in group photos and websites. But diversity is usually for appearance purposes only. Everyone must toe the social, cultural, political, theological line. Token minorities should be seen but not heard.

Randy Woodley's voice needs to be heard. There is no need to discount that Randy's voice is part of a chorus of voices arising from the context of the Native American community. Randy represents a welcome and necessary voice from a previously silenced and underrepresented voice in American Christianity. But more than merely a voice of Native American Christianity, Randy brings the power of his wisdom shaped by his many years of experience. A combination of an academic with impressive credentials — a former pastor, ministry leader, and social action–oriented grassroots organizer — Randy brings his life, his story, his experience, culture, education, and creativity to bear in offering shalom theology applicable to every context.

This book provides a thoroughly biblical account. Revealing a profound immersion in the Word of God and a serious reflection on Scripture, Randy generates a fully biblical theology. This theological depth is coupled with cultural sensitivity. Without question, Randy's reflections are applicable to the broader context — in fact, I would deem his reflections to be an absolute necessity at this historic moment in American Christianity. Randy offers truth from his particular context, but with relevance and application to all.

Shalom theology and the Harmony Way suggest what the world should be, reflecting the fullness and wholeness of God's creation. This book offers the great possibility as never before — that the North American church could reflect the reality of God's shalom, a shalom that is fully embodied rather than merely referenced or abstracted. The book offers an important challenge to western cultural captivity, revealing its deficiency. But Randy does not simply point fingers at what's wrong with the world. In the true spirit of the prophets, he asserts the truth and calls us to a particular faithful pursuit of that truth. He expresses the ultimate act of trust in extending to us a hospitality that invites us to journey with him toward a shalom theology.

I trust the direction that Randy Woodley leads me. As you are led on this important journey through this book, trust the gift from God that is this journey.

Soong-Chan Rah
Milton B. Engebretson Associate Professor of
   Church Growth and Evangelism
North Park Theological Seminary
Author of *The Next Evangelicalism: Freeing the Church*
   from Western Cultural Captivity

Author's Preface

This book draws its foundation for a Native American harmony ethic largely from discoveries made during work on my Ph.D. dissertation. I began my dissertation project, titled *The Harmony Way: Integrating Indigenous Values within Native North American Theology and Mission,* with a reasonable hunch that there may be a shared life-concept that is widespread among Native Americans related to well-being, or, to living and viewing life in harmony and balance.

While writing this book I have tried to be intentional not to demythologize nor remythologize our Native American life-ways. Like any other people group (or in the case of Native Americans, many groups), our values are not static. Being Native American has meant many things to Native Americans in different times. There is no universal Native American culture. However, many Native Americans share some common values and what I have begun to refer to in a generic sense as a widespread *Harmony Way* construct. The Harmony Way is common within many First Nations' worldviews. My concern during my doctoral dissertation was to discover if a Harmony Way–type construct is widespread among America's indigenous peoples and then to what degree common values might be shared within the construct, even today.

I set about the discovery of the literature by reading from both Native American and non-Native observers and writers, in various areas of study but primarily concentrating on religion, education, psychology, and anthropology. I found within the literature that others had attempted to group Native American values by an assortment of ways and means. The

Harmony Way concept I sought to learn more about was referenced often within lists of Native American values, but the context of a harmony ethic was one value among many. The Harmony Way was not well defined as a broad and binding construct in the literature.

Following the integration of the initial literature into what at that time I had determined as core Native American values, I felt I needed more clarification about indigenous well-being. In an effort to discover whether or not these values would be relevant to a current Harmony Way construct, I created a survey that would:

a. query respondents about their familiarity with a harmony construct in their own tribes;
b. without any prompting, invite respondents to name some of the values that are found within the harmony constructs they were familiar with;
c. test respondents' familiarity with the values I had compiled in the literature.

One hundred Native Americans from forty-five different tribal groups took the survey. A preliminary look at the survey data convinced me that my hunch about a widespread Harmony Way construct among Native Americans had merit. Prior to examining the survey data more closely, I interviewed eight Native American elders/spiritual leaders who I knew were familiar with their own tribal traditions and who, to some degree, knew their own language. I began the interviews by asking them to speak freely about any concept among their own tribe that helped them to keep life in harmony and balance. Again, my hunch about the prevalent understanding of a Harmony Way construct was confirmed during each of the interviews.

I then grouped the responses of the interviews into categories of values that seemed to emerge. I grouped these in broad categories that, by and large, substantiated the values found in the literature. I then integrated the values into a single set of ten core Native American values that, I propose, constitute a widespread Native American Harmony Way. My next step was to set about the task of describing these values using the data collected, extant literature, and my own recollections and experiences. Some of these values are specifically mentioned in this book.

A parallel theological construct I had sensed earlier, that also made sense in this project and that most resembled the Native American Harmony Way, was *shalom*. The ancient Semitic construct of shalom, particularly as it is understood by theologian Walter Brueggemann, seemed very similar to the Harmony Way. I discovered that in many ways, shalom and the Native American Harmony Way are interchangeable constructs. In my discovery I found that only a broad-based, yet concrete theological construct would be able to compare with the Native American Harmony Way. For instance, one could argue that love is broad based but love can be interpreted ambiguously. Shalom is broad based but is not ambiguous.

In their nature as constructs, shalom and the Native American Harmony Way have much in common. Shalom, like Harmony Way, is made up of numerous notions and values, with the *whole* being much greater than the sum of its parts. Both are meant to be a way of living life in concrete ways that include more than all the terms found within the construct. They both set forth practical steps included within a vision for living. They both require specific action when the harmony or shalom is broken. They both have justice, restoration, and continuous right living as their goal. And, perhaps most importantly, they both originate as *the* right path for living, being viewed as a gift from the Creator.

In this book I suggest that viewing the shalom construct through indigenous eyes can encourage in people a new way to experience theology and also provoke in them a fresh spiritual journey. Indigenous theological and spiritual views have often been overlooked in the past, considered to be outside the realm of mainstream theology; but now, they are providing challenges to the most fundamental theological constructs of the Christian faith from the inside. Central to many of these "new" alternative views (at least new to the metaphorical theological "table") is the foundational understanding of Native American well-being as a harmony construction. I would like to suggest, even more broadly, that many indigenous peoples around the world have constructs of shalom or harmony in their own constructs of well-being. If this is the case, and I believe it is the case, then Christians should give ear to what indigenous peoples have to say, especially in this day when Euro-western Christianity is so broken and fragmented. In fact, by listening to the spirituality and theology of indigenous peoples, Euro-western peoples might have saved themselves and others, and still can, from centuries of spiritual difficulty.

Native Americans have been the recipients of American church mission longer than any other people in the world. We have scrutinized the message and the messengers for centuries and we have something to say. My perspective is rooted in redemptive correction and my interest is in putting out a call for true partnership through the co-creation, not just of new theological ideas, but of a new theological system. Put in context, this book is one of the many responses Philip Jenkins in *The Next Christendom* told the west to expect. Jenkins speculated that the theologies of the twenty-first century would, by and large, come from the global South and East. Regrettably, Jenkins neglected to build the expectation for a unique and distinctive response from America's indigenous peoples. Then again, who would expect such a response after five hundred years of colonial mission?

Introduction

Similar to many other Americans today, my own relationship with creation has been stunted and marked by fits and starts.[1] Like every youngster, along with my siblings, cousins, and friends, I ran through the local woods, traversed open fields, picked apples from an unsuspecting neighbor's orchard, watched the birds, bees, and blossoms, lay in the grass, smelled the dirt, and spent time (mostly playing) in our family garden.

As a small child my most memorable experiences of relationship building with creation occurred during annual or semiannual visits to my southern grandparents' homes. Through those small eyes during visits to northeast Mississippi I learned that drinking water came from deep under the earth, and with a crank and a bucket I could draw the coldest, freshest, and sweetest water that I would ever taste. I learned about rabbit hunting and "leading your shot" by walking my grandfather's woods and fields with him. I was taught about fishing with a cane pole and bobber at my grandfather's pond. My father's parents (Mamaw and Papaw to me) raised their

---

1. I share my own childhood experiences, which are perhaps common to many other Americans, Native and non-Native, in an effort to dismiss the idea that all Native Americans love nature or have a special or mystical connection with creation. While it is true that indigenous cultures who have been least affected by modernity are likely to understand and know the stories of the land more than modern, immigrant peoples, this type of assumption can easily become a stereotype. You will notice in this book that I often try to qualify the stereotype by using terms like *indigenous* or *traditional* when referring to the connection between creation and Native Americans. After all, the purpose of the book is to assist *all peoples* in finding or recovering a sense of connectedness to creation via a shalom-type construct.

own garden crops, chickens, hogs, and cattle and knew how to watch the weather in order to survive. Through this southern world, creation opened her embrace to me, and I would sometimes find myself disappearing for hours just to listen to the creek flow or sense the trees and fields around me. Mississippi red clay really does have its own distinct smell and feel.

I felt something else on that land too. I knew the Chickasaws had once occupied it and I knew the stories about the local Civil War skirmishes that had overflowed from nearby battles onto the place that became home to my grandparents. The land had a story to tell and I had heard several narratives explaining the unique history of the area from the locals and my relatives. Sometimes I would sit alone for hours in the field near a branch or a pond, just trying to hear that particular story. There, near cotton fields that were once battlefields, the land spoke to me.

We also visited my maternal grandparents at least once a year. There, in north central Alabama, with full access to all my many uncles and aunties' jubilance and teasing, storytelling and guitar picking, I was shown how to catch rain, watch characteristics of certain birds, set a snare for fish, watch for snakes while swimming in the river, pick and prepare pokeweed, catch lightning bugs, frogs, and snakes, and even entertain myself by "flying June bugs" on a thread. Through my mother's relatives we also heard the stories of the land. It seemed like all my Alabama relatives were great storytellers. I particularly enjoyed it when my Grandma Love would share. Besides being the best lady to ever live (no exaggeration), her stories carried a mystique that caused us kids to listen to her intently. Those stories were real to me — some historical, some clearly fictional, but most falling into that mysterious category that even a child knew better than to classify too narrowly. Those stories and that land could not be separated. They didn't even make sense outside of that place, and that's what made my experiences so real.

I always looked forward to our family's southern jaunts because I found myself in those places, surrounded by my relatives in what we called "the country." I think in those early years I learned that the land was much more than "mere" land. Somehow I just knew, and "how" didn't really matter to me then; the land, water, skies, trees, animals, birds, and insects were all alive, just like me. I think because of those early experiences during various times in my life, regardless of age, I would always find myself returning to the security of God's bosom of creation. Regardless of how much of a street kid, "stoner," or student I would become, I always found my real home away from the reaches of concrete and artificial lights.

As an older teen, and later as a young adult, I spent many retreats fishing, hunting, backpacking, and hiking in the wilderness country, wherever I could find it. Most of the time these activities were just an excuse to get out and get away. I grew up in the land of the Huron and Ojibwa peoples. I tried to learn their story, both in school and through listening to the land. I owe a great debt to them. I think some of my fondest memories are of me, at various places in my early years in Michigan, just lying on the earth and feeling my own heartbeat blend with the gurgle of a stream, the songs of birds, and the chirps of squirrels.

Because I was at rest in creation, I often received signs from the Creator early in my life, confirming his presence and his concern for my well-being. Those signs and those stories are now numerous, and I have never felt the need to categorize them beyond a simple understanding that God is present in creation; and in this, there is a kind of harmony. In all our connection to the creation, there is a sense of shalom.

The first time I think I actually realized that some people felt alienated from creation was in 1980 when, for my job working with Denver juvenile delinquents, we took a dozen of them backpacking in Rocky Mountain National Park. Out on the trails these tough street kids acted as if they were truly "babes in the woods." I thought it strange that what I considered to be serene and peaceful, they were interpreting as chaos. That first night several of those "tough" urban kids broke down and cried like babies for their mothers. It took me a while to understand what they must have been experiencing.

Unfortunately, the experience of modern urban folks in America has become much closer to that of the alienated and frightened teenagers I knew, than one of shalom in the community of creation. We now find ourselves as the children of a modern technological society divorced from creation, only allowing visitations during summer camps, nature shows on television, or through accidental encounters such as glancing at the starry sky as we cross a parking lot.

The Creator is calling us back to experience God's love and care in the created world around us. The indigenous peoples of our own lands are the guides and theological interpreters of this too-long-awaited journey. Between my own mixed experiences as a child and having spent over half my adult life around indigenous communities, listening to indigenous elders, and so forth, I think I have found a kind of wisdom for living on this planet that transcends modernity's purview. This book is an introduction that will begin to prepare western hearts and minds for a journey, hopefully from which one will find it difficult to return. My hope is that once we begin to live out shalom in the community of creation, we will not want to return. It is time for the people of the earth to return to creation. In doing so, we may find the heart of the Creator once again in our own hearts.

CHAPTER ONE

Shalom: Greater Than the Sum of Its Parts

A Large Story

Shalom is a large concept that requires us to ask large questions. Shalom living is how life is meant to be. When we ask how life is meant to be we are also concerning ourselves with the how and why of life's purpose, such as, "Where do we all come from?" "How did evil come into the world?" "What is the relationship between human beings and the rest of creation?" "How should people live with one another?" Western philosophy tends to require precise definitions and prior knowledge in order to fully discuss what is common to us all. When delving into such cosmological realms it may be easier to ask our questions in the same way a child would ask them, rather than to think "philosophy."

I remember as a pastor, when it was my turn to do the children's story, I would begin by telling the adults present, "If you can understand the message through the children's story, feel free to leave before I give the adult sermon." Well, I don't think anyone ever left early, but more often than not people would remember what was said during the children's message better than what they recalled about the adult message. Among our Cherokee people we have stories that address the big questions of life. No one story deals with every big question, but the one I am about to share speaks to many cosmological concerns, not only for the Cherokee but for all human beings.[1]

---

1. There are different versions of this story, but this one, as recorded by anthropologist James Mooney, has the most detail.

1

(Note: Even if you fully understand this first story, please continue reading the rest of the book!)

Long years ago, soon after the world was made, a hunter and his wife lived at Pilot Knob with their only child, a little boy. The father's name was Kana'ti (Lucky Hunter), and his wife was called Selu (Corn). No matter when Kana'ti went into the woods, he never failed to bring back a load of game, which his wife would cut up and prepare, washing off the blood from the meat in the river near the house. The little boy used to play down by the river every day, and one morning the old people thought they heard laughing and talking in the bushes as though there were two children there. When the boy came home at night his parents asked him who had been playing with him all day. "He comes out of the water," said the boy, "and he calls himself my elder brother. He says his mother was cruel to him and threw him into the river." Then they knew that the strange boy had sprung from the blood of the game that Selu had washed off at the river's edge.

Every day when the little boy went out to play the other would join him, but as he always went back again into the water the old people never had a chance to see him. At last one evening Kana'ti said to his son, "Tomorrow, when the other boy comes to play, get him to wrestle with you, and when you have your arms around him hold on to him and call for us." The boy promised to do as he was told, so the next day as soon as his playmate appeared he challenged him to a wrestling match. The other agreed at once, but as soon as they had their arms around each other, Kana'ti's boy began to scream for his father. The old folks at once came running down, and as soon as the Wild Boy saw them he struggled to free himself and cried out, "Let me go; you threw me away!" but his brother held on until the parents reached the spot, when they seized the Wild Boy and took him home with them. They kept him in the house until they had tamed him, but he was always wild and artful in his disposition, and was the leader of his brother in every mischief. It was not long until the old people discovered that he had magic powers, and they called him I'nage-utasvhi (He-who-grew-up-wild).

Whenever Kana'ti went into the mountains he always brought back a fat buck or doe, or maybe a couple of turkeys. One day the Wild Boy said to his brother, "I wonder where our father gets all that game; let's follow him next time and find out." A few days afterward Kana'ti took a bow and some feathers in his hand and started off toward the west. The boys waited a little while and then went after him, keeping out of sight until they saw him go into a swamp where there were a great many of the small reeds that hunters use to make arrow shafts. Then the Wild Boy changed himself into a puff of bird's down, which the wind took up and carried until it alighted upon Kana'ti's shoulder just as he entered the swamp, but Kana'ti knew nothing about it. The old man cut reeds, fitted the feathers to them and made some arrows, and the Wild Boy — in his other shape — thought, "I wonder what those things are for." When Kana'ti had his arrows finished he came out of the swamp and went on again. The wind blew the down from his shoulder, and it fell in the woods, when the Wild Boy took his right shape again and went back and told his brother what he had seen. Keeping out of sight of their father, they followed him up the mountain until he stopped at a certain place and lifted a large rock. At once there ran out a buck, which Kana'ti shot, and then lifting it upon his back he started for home again. "Oho!" exclaimed the boys. "He keeps all the deer shut up in that hole, and whenever he wants meat he just lets one out and kills it with those things he made in the swamp." They hurried and reached home before their father, who had the heavy deer to carry, and he never knew that they had followed.

A few days later the boys went back to the swamp, cut some reeds, and made seven arrows, and then started up the mountain to where their father kept the game. When they got to the place, they raised the rock and a deer came running out. Just as they drew back to shoot it, another came out, and then another and another, until the boys got confused and forgot what they were about. In those days all the deer had their tails hanging down like other animals, but as a buck was running past the Wild Boy struck its tail with his arrow so that it pointed upward. The boys thought this good sport, and when the next one ran past the Wild Boy struck its tail so that it too stood straight up, and his brother struck the next one so hard with his arrow that the deer's tail was almost curled over his back. The deer carries his tail this way ever since. The deer came running past until the last one had come out of the hole and escaped into the forest. Then came droves of raccoons, rabbits, and all the other four-footed animals — all but the bear, because there were no bear then. Last came great flocks of turkeys, pigeons, and partridges that darkened the air like a cloud and made such a noise with their wings that Kana'ti, sitting at home, heard the sound like distant thunder on the mountains and said to himself, "My bad boys have got into trouble; I must go and see what they are doing."

So he went up the mountain, and when he came to the place where he kept the game he found the two boys standing by the rock, and all the birds and animals were gone. Kana'ti was furious, but without saying a word he went down into the cave and kicked the covers off four jars in one corner. Out swarmed bedbugs, fleas, lice, and gnats, and got all over the boys. They screamed with pain and fright and tried to beat off the insects, but the thousands of vermin crawled over them and bit and stung them until both dropped down nearly dead. Kana'ti stood looking on until he thought they had been punished enough; then he knocked off the vermin and gave the boys a lecture. "Now, you rascals," said he, "you have always had plenty to eat and never had to work for it. Whenever you were hungry all I had to do was to come up here and get a deer or a turkey and bring it home for your mother to cook; but now you have let out all the animals, and after this when you want a deer to eat you will have to hunt all over the woods for it, and then maybe not find one. Go home now to your mother, while I see if I can find something to eat for supper."

When the boys got home again they were very tired and hungry and asked their mother for something to eat. "There is no meat," said Selu, "but wait a little while and I'll get you something." So she took a basket and started out to the storehouse. This storehouse was built upon poles high up from the ground, to keep it out of the reach of animals, and there was a ladder to climb up by, and one door, but no other opening. Every day when Selu got ready to cook the dinner she would go out to the storehouse with a basket and bring it back full of corn and beans. The boys had never been inside the storehouse, so they wondered where all the corn and beans could come from, as the house was not a very large one; so as soon as Selu went out of the door the Wild Boy said to his brother, "Let's go and see what she does." They ran around and climbed up at the back of the storehouse and pulled out a piece of clay from between the logs, so that they could look in. There they saw Selu standing in the middle of the room with the basket in front of her on the floor. Leaning over the basket, she rubbed her stomach — *so* — and the basket was half full of corn. Then she rubbed under her armpits — *so* — and the basket was full to the top with beans. The boys looked at each other and said, "This will never do; our mother is a witch. If we eat any of that it will poison us. We must kill her."

4

When the boys came back into the house, she knew their thoughts before they spoke. "So you are going to kill me?" said Selu. "Yes," said the boys. "You are a witch." "Well," said their mother, "when you have killed me, clear a large piece of ground in front of the house and drag my body seven times around the circle. Then drag me seven times over the ground inside the circle, and stay up all night and watch, and in the morning you will have plenty of corn." The boys killed her with their clubs, and cut off her head and put it up on the roof of the house with her face turned to the west, and told her to look for her husband. Then they set to work to clear the ground in front of the house, but instead of clearing the whole piece they cleared only seven little spots. This is why corn now grows only in a few places instead of over the whole world. They dragged the body of Selu around the circle, and wherever her blood fell on the ground the corn sprang up. But instead of dragging her body seven times across the ground they dragged it over only twice, which is the reason the people still work their crop but twice. The two brothers sat up and watched their corn all night, and in the morning it was full grown and ripe.

When Kana'ti came home at last, he looked around, but could not see Selu anywhere, and asked the boys where their mother was. "She was a witch, and we killed her," said the boys. "There is her head up there on top of the house." When he saw his wife's head on the roof, he was very angry, and said, "I won't stay with you any longer; I am going to the Wolf people." So he started off, but before he had gone far the Wild Boy changed himself again to a tuft of down, which fell on Kana'ti's shoulder. When Kana'ti reached the settlement of the Wolf people, they were holding a council in the townhouse. He went in and sat down with the tuft of bird's down on his shoulder, but he never noticed it. When the Wolf chief asked him his business, he said: "I have two bad boys at home, and I want you to go in seven days from now and play ball against them." Although Kana'ti spoke as though he wanted them to play a game of ball, the Wolves knew that he meant for them to go and kill the two boys. They promised to go. Then the bird's down blew off from Kana'ti's shoulder, and the smoke carried it up through the hole in the roof of the townhouse. When it came down on the ground outside, the Wild Boy took his right shape again and went home and told his brother all that he had heard in the townhouse. But when Kana'ti left the Wolf people, he did not return home, but went on farther.

5

The boys then began to get ready for the Wolves, and the Wild Boy — the magician — told his brother what to do. They ran around the house in a wide circle until they had made a trail all around it except on the side from which the Wolves would come, where they left a small open space. Then they made four large bundles of arrows and placed them at four different points on the outside of the circle, after which they hid themselves in the woods and waited for the Wolves. In a day or two a whole party of Wolves came and surrounded the house to kill the boys. The Wolves did not notice the trail around the house, because they came in where the boys had left the opening, but the moment they went inside the circle the trail changed to a high brush fence and shut them in. Then the boys on the outside took their arrows and began shooting them down, and as the Wolves could not jump over the fence they were all killed, excepting a few that escaped through the opening into a great swamp close by. The boys ran around the swamp, and a circle of fire sprang up in their tracks and set fire to the grass and bushes and burned up nearly all the other Wolves. Only two or three got away, and from these have come all the wolves that are now in the world.

Soon afterward some strangers from a distance, who had heard that the brothers had a wonderful grain from which they made bread, came to ask for some, for none but Selu and her family had ever known corn before. The boys gave them seven grains of corn, which they told them to plant the next night on their way home. If they sat up all night to watch the corn, they would have seven ripe ears in the morning. These they were to plant the next night and watch in the same way, and so on every night until they reached home, when they would have corn enough to supply the whole people. The strangers lived seven days' journey away. They took the seven grains and watched all through the darkness until morning, when they saw seven tall stalks, each stalk bearing a ripened ear. They gathered the ears and went on their way. The next night they planted all their corn, and guarded it as before until daybreak, when they found an abundant increase. But the way was long and the sun was hot, and the people grew tired. On the last night before reaching home they fell asleep, and in the morning the corn they had planted had not even sprouted. They brought with them to their settlement what corn they had left and planted it. With care and attention they were able to raise a crop. But ever since, the corn must be watched and tended through half the year, which before would grow and ripen in a night.

When Kana'ti did not return, the boys at last decided to go and find him. The Wild Boy took a gaming wheel and rolled it toward the Darkening land. In a little while the wheel came rolling back, and the boys knew their father was not there. He rolled it to the south and to the north. Each time the wheel came back to him, and they knew their father was not there. Then he rolled it toward the Sun Land, and it did not return. "Our father is there," said the Wild Boy. "Let us go and find him." So the two brothers set off toward the east, and after traveling a long time they came upon Kana'ti walking along with a little dog by his side. "You bad boys," said their father. "You have found me when I didn't want to see you again." "Yes," they answered. "We always accomplish what we start out to do — we are men." "This dog overtook me four days ago," Kana'ti said, but the boys knew that the dog was the wheel they had sent after him to find him. "Well," said Kana'ti, "as long as you have found me, we may as well travel together, but I shall take the lead."

Soon they came to a swamp, and Kana'ti told them there was something dangerous there and they must keep away from it. He went on ahead, but as soon as he was out of sight the Wild Boy said to his brother, "Come and let us see what is in the swamp." They went in together, and in the middle of the swamp, they found a large panther asleep. The Wild Boy got out an arrow and shot the panther in the side of the head. The panther turned his head and the other boy shot him on that side. He turned his head away again and the two brothers shot together — *tust, tust, tust!* But the panther was not hurt by the arrows and paid no more attention to the boys. They came out of the swamp and soon overtook Kana'ti, waiting for them. "Did you find it?" asked Kana'ti. "Yes," said the boys. "We found it, but it never hurt us. We are men." Kana'ti was surprised, but said nothing, and they went on again.

After a while he turned to them and said, "Now you must be careful. We are coming to a tribe called the Anada'dvtaski ('Roasters'), and if they get you they will put you into a pot and feast on you." Then he went on ahead. Soon the boys came to a tree that had been struck by lightning, and the Wild Boy directed his brother to gather some of the splinters from the tree and told him what to do with them. In a little while they came to the settlement of the cannibals, who, as soon as they saw the boys, came running out, crying, "Good, here are two nice fat strangers. Now we'll have a grand feast! They caught the boys and dragged them into the townhouse, and sent word to all the people of

7

the settlement to come to the feast. They made up a great fire, put water into a large pot and set it to boiling, and then seized the Wild Boy and put him down into it. His brother was not in the least frightened and made no attempt to escape, but quietly knelt down and began putting the splinters into the fire, as if to make it burn better. When the cannibals thought the meat was about ready they lifted the pot from the fire, and that instant a blinding light filled the townhouse, and lightning began to dart from one side to the other, striking down the cannibals until not one of them was left alive. Then the lightning went up through the smoke-hole, and the next moment the two boys were standing outside the townhouse as though nothing had happened. They went on and soon met Kana'ti, who seemed much surprised to see them, and said, "What! Are you here again?" "Oh, yes, we never give up. We are great men!" "What did the cannibals do to you?" "We met them and they brought us to their townhouse, but they never hurt us." Kana'ti said nothing more, and they went on.

He soon got out of sight of the boys, but they kept on until they came to the end of the world, where the sun comes out. The sky was just coming down when they got there, but they waited until it went up again, and then they went through and climbed up on the other side. There they found Kana'ti and Selu sitting together. The old folk received them kindly and were glad to see them, telling them they might stay there a while, but then they must go to live where the sun goes down. The boys stayed with their parents seven days and then went on toward the Darkening land, where they are now. We call them Anisga'ya Tsunsdi' (the Little Men), and when they talk to each other we hear low rolling thunder in the west.

After Kana'ti's boys had let the deer out of the cave where their father used to keep them, the hunters tramped about in the woods for a long time without finding any game, so that the people were very hungry. At last they heard that the Thunder Boys were now living in the far west, beyond the sun door, and that if they were sent for they could bring back the game. So they sent messengers for them, and the boys came and sat down in the middle of the townhouse and began to sing.

At the first song there was a roaring sound like a strong wind in the northwest, and it grew louder and nearer as the boys sang on, until at the seventh song a whole herd of deer, led by a large buck, came out of the woods. The boys had told the people to be ready with their bows and arrows, and when the song was ended and all the deer were close around the townhouse, the hunters shot into them and killed as many as they needed before the herd could get back into the timber. Then the Thunder Boys went back to the Darkening land, but before they left they taught the people the seven songs with which to call up the deer. It all happened so long ago that the songs are now forgotten — all but two, which the hunters still sing whenever they go after deer.[2]

Although there are many areas addressed by the story, at this time I simply want to draw your attention to the relationship between the human beings, animals, and plants. There is a symbiotic connection between the origin of the Wild Boy and the meat provided in a similar way, and between Corn Woman and the corn and beans. The former is made from the blood drained from the meat; the other produces food, both from her body and the seeds she leaves. In the case of the Hunter and Corn Woman, food was provided as a gift, but later, the gift would need to be sought with more effort. The gifts of the earth, supplied by the Creator, became costly, though still considered as gifts. In the end, the family was reunited, harmony was restored, and the benefits of the restoration were passed down to the generations who followed.

In our day we desperately need a restoration of harmony between human beings, the Creator, the earth, and all God provides through the earth such as plants and animals. Many species of plants and animals are going extinct at an alarming rate. Much of our fresh water is being made into a commodity while what is available is often unfit to drink or fish. Seafood is tainted and disappearing; urban development is ever widening, draining precious wetlands and forcing small farmers out of business. The bulk of our meat and vegetables is genetically modified, mostly grown on horrific industrial farm-factories and tainted by harmful chemicals. Today, the relationship between human beings, plants, and animals has been damaged tremendously and we are just now beginning to count the cost of abusing the precious gifts that the Creator has so abundantly supplied. A renewed understanding of living out shalom on earth, and the equivalent constructs found among indigenous peoples, is our path to restoring harmony in the world.

---

2. James Mooney, *Myths of the Cherokee* (New York: Dover, 1995), 242-48, and originally published by the U.S. Government Printing Office, Washington, D.C., in 1900 as *Nineteenth Annual Report of the Bureau of American Ethnology to the Secretary of the Smithsonian Institute.*

Shalom, More Than Peace

Shalom is a Hebrew word, often used in the Scriptures to mean "peace," right? That's correct only if you consider it correct to call the Grand Canyon "a large crack in the ground" or the Pacific Ocean "a large pool of water." Shalom is much more than just a "large" term. There is likely as much residual breadth and depth to the meaning of shalom as there is residual expanse or residual water in the meanings of the aforementioned examples. Not only does shalom express much more than "peace," but the kind of peace shalom represents is active and engaged, going far beyond the mere absence of conflict. A fuller understanding of shalom is the key to the door that can lead us to a whole new way of living in our world. As Terry McGonigal explains,

> Although the word "peace" (Hebrew: *shalom,* Greek: *eirene*) appears over 500 times in scripture, this theme and its implications have been overlooked in biblical theology. God's design for and delight in diversity are embedded in the creation narratives, which describe order, relationships, stewardship, beauty and rhythm as the essential foundations for shalom, "the way God designed the universe to be."[3]

According to McGonigal, the biblical shalom construct should be understood as both natural and in every respect, God's very Way, existing in and through all creation. There is a wide array of words and theological examples of shalom that give depth and flavor to the simple English word "peace," as it is used in the Scriptures. Examples of various aspects of shalom include, according to one concordance,[4] completeness, wholeness, health, peace, welfare, safety, soundness, tranquility, prosperity, perfectness, fullness, rest, harmony, and the absence of agitation or discord. Another concordance lists the word origin of *shalom* from *shalem,* meaning completeness, soundness, welfare, and peace and repayment. Words used to translate *shalem* in the NASB include close, ease, favorable, friend, friendly terms, friends, greet, greeted, health, peace, peaceably, peaceful, peacefully, perfect peace, prosperity, safe, safely, safety, secure, trusted, welfare, well, well-being, and wholly.[5]

3. Terry McGonigal, *"If You Only Knew What Would Bring Peace": Shalom Theology as the Biblical Foundation for Diversity* (Unpublished, 2010), 2. Used with permission.

4. James Strong, *Strong's Exhaustive Concordance of the Bible with Greek and Hebrew Dictionaries* (Nashville: Royal Publishers, 1979), no. 7965.

5. *The NAS Exhaustive Concordance of the Bible with Hebrew-Aramaic and Greek Dic-*

In the Second Testament, the term *eirene* is used to mean "peace"; but again, Semitic writers of the New Testament would have likely understood its Hebrew correspondent to include the larger construct. Such a rich list of descriptors leans heavily into the concepts of love, justice, and God's created intention, concepts that truly make the word *shalom* a profound construction.

A New World Order

Imagine, if you will, a new world order that has the power to enforce a decree stating we must live by all the words and concepts in the lists above. Such an action would change our world drastically. In this new world, historic wrongs would be righted; former enemies would come back together in love; through restitution, justice would be served to those who had been wronged for years; people with physical, emotional, mental, and spiritual afflictions and anguish would be healed; people would be at peace with one another; beasts would no longer stalk humans; plants would no longer be poisonous to us; pollution would cease; climate change would be thwarted; there would be no wars; and everyone and everything would be happy with the Creator and all creation.

Such images are not utopian in nature; as God's intentions for all creation they are supposed to be reality. We need not think that such a world could only exist in the human imagination, because the Creator has embedded this desire deep within the core of our being. The Scriptures are replete with words and images of what such a world should look like. God's preferred order of existence for our world is shown by such images in Scripture as the garden of Eden, the Sabbath system, and Jubilee. Other shalom descriptions come to mind from the prophets, such as God's Holy Mountain and the Great Day of the Lord. Images of shalom in the Second Testament concern the advent of the Messiah, the kingdom of God, and the church.[6] The Scriptures brim with images of and references to shalom.

---

tionaries (The Lockman Foundation, 1981, 1998). See also Ludwig Koehler, Walter Baumgartner, and Johann J. Stamm, *The Hebrew and Aramaic Lexicon of the Old Testament: The New Koehler and Baumgartner in English,* trans. M. E. Richardson (Leiden: E. J. Brill, 1993-).

6. I assert that there is enough continuity in all the biblical constructs of shalom images and words, for the various writers to understand a crucial, national, and sometimes universal shalom motif. It may even be argued that shalom is the metanarrative of the Torah. The Talmud states, "The entire Torah is for the sake of the ways of shalom" (Talmud, Gittin

But even the proper understanding of shalom simply as peace, exemplified below by Isaiah, is much greater than a mere absence of conflict.

> Many peoples shall come and say,
> "Come, let us go up to the mountain of the LORD,
> to the house of the God of Jacob;
> that he may teach us his ways
> and that we may walk in his paths."
> For out of Zion shall go forth instruction,
> and the word of the LORD from Jerusalem.
> He shall judge between the nations,
> and shall arbitrate for many peoples;
> they shall beat their swords into ploughshares,
> and their spears into pruning-hooks;
> nation shall not lift up sword against nation,
> neither shall they learn war any more. (Isa. 2:3-4)

Isaiah visualized a world where all the nations on earth would learn from the Creator how to enact true peace. The result of such learning means that peace could be the norm. So much so, that all the weapons of warfare in the world could be melted down into useful tools in order to be used for feeding the world's population. Not only does shalom, understood here as peace, accomplish the task of ending the bloodshed, but it appropriates the old war-making resources to solve the problem of world hunger. In such a world tanks, missiles, fighter jets, nuclear devices, smart bombs, and all other military weaponry would be recycled into useful, job-producing, and food-producing implements. Imagine driving a tank into a processing line and watching formerly unemployed people transform it into a tractor. Isaiah continues his understanding of shalom in peace trajectory in the following passage.

> The wolf shall live with the lamb,
> the leopard shall lie down with the kid,

59b). Again in the Mishneh: "Great is shalom, as the whole Torah was given in order to promote shalom in the world, as it is stated, 'Her ways are pleasant ways and all her paths are shalom'" (Maimonides, Mishneh Torah, The Laws of Chanukah 4:14). Working from a christocentric hermeneutic, I will show heuristically how I believe Jesus concurred with the understanding of shalom as the primary motif in the Hebrew Testament, and how Christ was viewed afterwards, in the New Testament, as the fulfillment of the same shalom motif. In other words, in the Second Testament, Christ fulfills the scriptural shalom metanarrative.

the calf and the lion and the fatling together,
and a little child shall lead them.
The cow and the bear shall graze,
their young shall lie down together;
and the lion shall eat straw like the ox.
The nursing child shall play over the hole of the asp,
and the weaned child shall put its hand on the adder's den.
They will not hurt or destroy
on all my holy mountain;
for the earth will be full of the knowledge of the LORD
as the waters cover the sea. (Isa. 11:6-9)

Here, the prophet uses the image of children playing in the midst of wild beasts and deadly vipers to make the point that shalom means safety and security. Isaiah conjures up the images of the most deadly beast of his day and sets the people's progeny (their children) and their livelihood (sheep, goats, and cattle) among them.

Perhaps Isaiah is tweaking his image of shalom through the use of hyperbole, but nothing could be more frightening or more real to people living in a pastoral economy than exposing the things they value most to the things they fear most. In such an economy the point of wealth (as blessing) is the ability to secure livestock and land for one's progeny. Isaiah's point is well taken; shalom existence is based in a newfound security. In such a world of shalom as peace and security, we neither have to war anymore, nor do we need to exercise the daily worries over our children or livelihood. In shalom, warring over turf, wealth, or national security are extinct practices. In shalom, family wealth is no longer the point of blessing because living out shalom offers an alternative way for people to view wealth. The concept of blessing in a world based upon shalom is shalom itself.

As I mentioned, the Second Testament is also full of ways of describing shalom as peace. Second Testament imagery includes descriptors such as a body, with each part serving the other; a building, with each brick fitting the other; a new peaceable kingdom, with Jesus being the fulfillment of former images, to the point where he is named not only as the shalom bringer, but as shalom itself, "for he himself is our peace" (Eph. 2:14a NIV). Paul's reference in Ephesians 2 may be drawing from the logical background of Judges 6:24a (NLT): "And Gideon built an altar to the LORD there and named it Yahweh-Shalom (which means 'the LORD is peace')."

The writer of Colossians, presumably the apostle Paul, makes the transcendent connection with shalom by sharing the ways Christians should be treating one another in a shalom-based world. Paul's understanding of peace, and its antecedent shalom, is noticeable when one considers the ways he describes just how followers of Christ should live. Nowhere do Paul's views seem to be more in step with other scriptural actions of shalom.

> Since God chose you to be the holy people he loves, you must clothe yourselves with tenderhearted mercy, kindness, humility, gentleness, and patience. Make allowance for each other's faults, and forgive anyone who offends you. Remember, the Lord forgave you, so you must forgive others. Above all, clothe yourselves with love, which binds us all together in perfect harmony. And let the [shalom] that comes from Christ rule in your hearts. For as members of one body you are called to live in [shalom]. And always be thankful. (Col. 3:12-15 NLT)

Again, like the Ephesians 2 passage, the image Paul creates in the above Colossians passage is one where shalom comes from Christ and one where Christ empowers us to live out shalom. Paul views the list of virtues, not as abstract moral commands, but as ways of describing people living out a shalom way of life.

At first glance all the images and the great list of words put together do not convey the full meaning of shalom. The Creator has ingeniously designed a world in which shalom is the foundational stuff that God uses to create proper order to the world. Put simply, shalom is originally located in God. Shalom is what we are to utilize each day as God lives through us. The responsibility of us as human caretakers of shalom living is to take these images, words, injunctions, and metaphors and apply them to our daily lives and to our world.

Shalom is meant to be both personal (emphasizing our relationships with others) and structural (replacing systems where shalom has been broken or which produce broken shalom, such as war- or greed-driven economic systems). In shalom, the old structures and systems are replaced with new structures and new systems. The universal expectation for all humanity to live out shalom has been given. Shalom has been decreed. God expects us to make the old way of living new. The Creator requires us to reshape the world we know into the world God has intended.

Shalom, Always Tested on the Margins

The task of creating communities where shalom is lived out may not be easy, but we can know whether or not we are successful in our efforts. How can a community tell if it is practicing shalom? Fortunately, a consistent standard is given throughout the sacred Scriptures. Shalom is always tested on the margins of a society and revealed by how the poor, oppressed, disempowered, and needy are treated. A huge gap between the wealthy and the poor may be a good indicator of the lack of shalom. Large discrepancies between wealth and poverty tend to lead to social oppression through injustice, which leads to other social ills like false imprisonment and disproportionate imprisoned populations of the marginalized (like minorities), unemployment, disproportionate military service by the poor and marginalized groups, high taxes (to support imperialism and the military), the opulence of the wealthy (and corporate tax welfare), children growing up without one or both parents, homelessness, prostitution, hunger, etcetera. These same social dynamics have remained unchanged in societies for thousands of years. As Jeremiah 5:28 notes in his day, "They have grown fat and sleek. They know no limits in deeds of wickedness; they do not judge with justice the cause of the orphan, to make it prosper, and they do not defend the rights of the needy."

A society concerned with shalom will care for the most marginalized among them. God has a special concern for the poor and needy, because how we treat them reveals our hearts, regardless of the rhetoric we employ to make ourselves sound just. Jeremiah 22:16 (NLT) equates the social task of caring to revealing a genuine relationship with God: "[King Josiah] gave justice and help to the poor and needy, and everything went well for him. 'Isn't that what it means to know me?' says the LORD."

Even a society with the abuse of wealth can find ways to meet the needs of the most needy among them. If not, the problem becomes systemic and eventually everyone, even the nonwealthy, are considered by God to be culpable. If injustice is left unchecked, "Even common people oppress the poor, rob the needy, and deprive foreigners of justice," according to Ezekiel 22:29 (NLT). Amos 5:12 describes systemic oppression of the poor like this: "For I know the vast number of your sins and the depth of your rebellions. You oppress good people by taking bribes and deprive the poor of justice in the courts." And again in Amos 8:4-5 (NLT): "Listen to this, you who rob the poor and trample down the needy! You can't wait for the Sabbath day to be over and the religious festivals to end so you can get back to cheating the helpless. You measure out grain with dishonest measures and cheat the buyer with dishonest scales." Injustice against the poor reveals our own state of shalom and the posture God takes for us or against us.

Widows, orphans, and foreigners/strangers/resident aliens (depending on translation) appear as a triad throughout the Hebrew Testament representing the concerns of the poor, needy, downtrodden, oppressed, and disempowered. Why? In a patriarchal society the needs of these three are more apparent than others. A woman who has lost her husband has also lost all her legal and social standing. She is at the mercy of society. An orphan, having suffered a traumatic loss, is without an inheritance because he/she has no father and therefore no future. A foreigner, perhaps homeless from war or tragedy, is considered an outsider with no family ties and therefore no means of inheritance. A stranger does not know the ways of the people and is not easily trusted, so God commands immediate hospitality and eventual full acceptance for such people. The *disempowered triad* of widows, orphans, and strangers best represent God's concern for those who have few material goods (food, clothing, shelter) and who are most easily oppressed (justice). Shalom addresses God's concern for the socially marginalized.

In the culture of the garden of Eden, God provided all that humanity needed for survival through the superabundance of nature. The state of the garden was blessed. In a post-Eden state, as people formed more complex governments, enacted inheritance laws, and delineated justice systems, the potential for abuse became much greater. God commands that every society have a safety net for those who "fall through the cracks." Individual care and generosity do not always take care of the poor and needy, so there must be a place for the needy built into the system that does care for them.

God provides for the needy in laws concerning agricultural work, through the Sabbath and Jubilee system, and through festivals and celebrations. Embedded in the command for Israel to tithe is God's concern for the poor: "Every third year you shall bring out the full tithe of your produce for that year, and store it within your towns; the Levites, because they have no allotment or inheritance with you, as well as the resident aliens, the orphans, and the widows in your towns, may come and eat their fill so that the LORD your God may bless you in all the work that you undertake" (Deut. 14:28-29).

The disempowered triad was meant to be so much a part of Israel's thinking that one need only mention one of the three to bring up the imagery of all three — and God's pressing concern for all the poor and marginalized. Widows, orphans, and strangers were hot-button words among the Jewish people as they worked out their own righteousness. The understanding of Israel's obligation to the poor, the marginalized, the oppressed widows, orphans, and strangers was meant to be so much a part of their thinking that God even commands them to leave any forgotten act of harvesting to benefit the poor.

> When you are harvesting your crops and forget to bring in a bundle of grain from your field, don't go back to get it. Leave it for the foreigners, orphans, and widows. Then the LORD your God will bless you in all you do. When you beat the olives from your olive trees, don't go over the boughs twice. Leave the remaining olives for the foreigners, orphans, and widows. When you gather the grapes in your vineyard, don't glean the vines after they are picked. Leave the remaining grapes for the foreigners, orphans, and widows. (Deut. 24:19-21)

God commands both individuals and the society in which they live to be generous and always take care of the poor. In such a community, shalom has a chance to thrive. In such a community, God will actually be glad to assign his name and dwell. "Then celebrate the Festival of Weeks to the LORD your God by giving a freewill offering in proportion to the blessings the LORD your God has given you. And rejoice before the LORD your God at the place he will choose as a dwelling for his Name — you, your sons and daughters, your male and female servants, the Levites in your towns, and the foreigners, the fatherless and the widows living among you" (Deut. 16:10-11 NIV). Why would God expect Israel to live out shalom in this way, and even maintain a grateful and appreciative attitude? The answer is revealed in the following verse: "Remember that you were slaves in Egypt, and follow carefully these decrees." God's intention was that Israel use their unfortunate circumstances, the time of slavery in Egypt when they had nothing, to check their attitude toward the poor and marginalized.[7] The Creator's concern for shalom communities to be built on justice and care for the poor went past Israel and stretched to all the boundaries of the earth.

---

7. For more on widows, orphans, and strangers see Deuteronomy 24:17; 26:12; 27:19; Job 22:9; Psalm 146:9; Jeremiah 22:3; Isaiah 1:16-18; Ezekiel 22:7; Zechariah 7:10; Malachi 3:5; and Acts 6:1.

God's Big Dream

The ancient Israelites are not the only people to have been given the Creator's construct of shalom as a formula for a good society. In Romans 1:20 Paul says that Gentiles, as well as Jews, can see the Creator through the creation. "Ever since the creation of the world his eternal power and divine nature, invisible though they are, have been understood and seen through the things he has made. So they are without excuse." Other ancient societies, from all parts of the world, have been given shalom-type constructs. There is so much we have to learn from the Creator simply through learning what God has done and is doing in creation. In the Genesis 1 account of creation, which I will explore later, we will see that shalom is clearly written in what God has created.

Paul also mentions, in Romans 2:15, the Law (Torah) written on our hearts. "They [the Gentiles] show that what the law requires is written on their hearts, to which their own conscience also bears witness; and their conflicting thoughts will accuse or perhaps excuse them." Neither nature or our own hearts excuse us from living according to the way God has intended. All around us, we have the Torah of creation. We have within our own hearts the Torah of conscience. We all know how to live out shalom.

How did Jesus describe what was required to live for God? "[Jesus] said to [the lawyer], 'You shall love the Lord your God with all your heart, and with all your soul, and with all your mind.' This is the greatest and first commandment. And a second is like it: 'You shall love your neighbor as yourself.' On these two commandments hang all the law and the prophets" (Matt. 22:37-40). The Law as interpreted by Jesus here is completely consistent with living out shalom. Many Native Americans understand the wisdom of living out shalom because it is a parallel concept to the harmony way of living that was given to our own people. We see harmony reflected in creation. We notice our own hearts have power to align with God's intended ways of living. We know, as all people know, to honor the Creator and treat others in the way we want to be treated.

In my doctoral dissertation I demonstrated how the Native American Harmony Way, though called different names by different tribes, is a widespread concept all across North America. After making my initial investigation into the Harmony Way, I discovered that the construct is much more widespread than I had at first imagined. Indigenous peoples from other places share similar constructs parallel to our understanding of harmony and the ancient Semitic understanding of shalom.

In my own relationships with other indigenes, I have heard similar testimonies of a type of harmony way of living and understanding life — from Zulu, Inca, Maasai, Sami, Maori, Inuit, Australian Aboriginal, and Hawaiian peoples. I don't think it is an understatement to say that the ancient Semitic shalom construct, or what we can broadly refer to as the Harmony Way, is the Creator's original instruction for the way in which all societies should be ordered, and for how all life on this planet should be lived.

The universality of shalom is what Old Testament scholar Walter Brueggemann describes when he says, "The central vision of world history in the Bible is that all of creation is one, every creature in community with every other, living in harmony and security toward the joy and well-being of every other creature."[8] This description reveals the connectedness of all creation and the resultant harmony and joy that come by realizing that connectedness. In the Hebrew Scriptures shalom is ubiquitous. Shalom is a very broad theological construct, but once understood it is like that missing tooth your tongue continually searches out; one can read again the Scriptures and find numerous shalom inferences and references from Genesis to Revelation. Brueggemann's view of the intimacy and the connectedness of all creation found within shalom[9] is consistent with many indigenous concepts of well-being. Indigenous people understand all parts of creation as related to one another.

Brueggemann goes on to say,

> That persistent vision of joy, well-being, harmony and prosperity is not captured in any single word or idea in the Bible; a cluster of words is required to express its many dimensions and subtle nuances: love, loyalty, truth, grace, salvation, justice, blessings, righteousness. But the term that in recent discussions has been used to summarize that controlling vision is *shalom*. Both in such discussion and in the Bible itself, it bears tremendous freight — the freight of a dream of God that resists all our tendencies to division, hostility, fear, drivenness, and misery. *Shalom* is the substance of the biblical vision of one community embracing all creation. It refers to all

8. Walter Brueggemann, *Peace: Living Toward a Vision* (St. Louis: Chalice Press, 2001), 13.

9. Brueggemann has done a wonderful job of explaining the broad concept of shalom. His understanding of shalom and the Native American constructs of harmony, such as found in quotes like the one I just listed, have numerous points in common.

those resources and factors that make communal harmony joyous and effective.[10]

In trying to simplify the ingenuity and theological grandeur of shalom we might ask ourselves a few elemental questions such as: How does God live? What holds the Trinity together? On what principles was the universe built? Put simply, shalom is the answer to such questions. Another question we might ask, reflecting Brueggemann's point, is this: *What is God's dream?* I believe our best attempt at understanding shalom says that God's dream is a world in which all creation lives in accordance with the way of shalom. The observation that all creation is connected not only suggests familiarity between all creation, but also expresses tangible and intentional relationships. In such relationships human beings should make room for the possibility that all creation, in some way, bears the image of the Creator. In other words, there is something of God in all of creation. Living out these relationships as sacred is living in shalom.

Native American Harmony as Shalom

As a result of the colonial enterprise, most indigenous communities are quite broken and fragmented. In one sense, we are like the "canary in the coal mine" for the Euro-western colonial experiment. Native Americans, like all of humanity, are in desperate need of living out a concept of healing and wholeness that includes a real partnership with creation. When I first studied shalom and the Native American Harmony Way, I wondered if these two concepts working in tandem could serve the purpose of restoration among our indigenous peoples. Later, I came to realize that the two constructs are essentially one and that all humanity has the same desperate need of healing, because God has designed us all to live in a world of shalom.

We are all in need of God's vision. Anything less than God's vision is broken shalom. Some broken systems exist that no longer serve the purpose of the common good but instead emanate injustice and unrighteousness. Says Brueggemann, "The consequences of justice and righteousness is *shalom,* an enduring Sabbath of joy and well-being. But the alternative is injustice and oppression, which lead inevitably to turmoil and anxiety,

10. Brueggemann, *Peace,* 14.

with no chance of well-being."[11] Turmoil and anxiety are hallmarks of our world. Brueggemann's understanding is incredibly similar to Native American concepts of broken harmony. Sometimes Native Americans refer to this broken state as a "broken hoop" or "broken circle."

A circle or a hoop is a tangible object that you can picture in your mind. Sometimes it can be difficult to get our heads around a concept, making it impractical to confront and address. Shalom is by no means intangible. Brueggemann points to the practicality of shalom:

> The Bible is not romantic about its vision. It never assumes shalom will come naturally or automatically. Indeed, there are many ways of compromising God's will for shalom. One way the community can say no to the vision and live without shalom is to deceive itself into thinking that its private arrangements of injustice and exploitation are suitable ways of living. . . . The prophetic vision of shalom stands against all private arrangements, all "separate peaces," all ghettos that pretend the others are not there (compare Luke 16:19-31). Religious legitimacy in the service of self-deceiving well-being is a form of chaos. Shalom is never the private property of the few.[12]

Shalom is communal, holistic, and tangible. There is no private or partial shalom. The whole community must have shalom or no one has shalom. As long as there are hungry people in a community that is well fed, there can be no shalom. Where there are homeless and jobless people amidst the employed and wealthy, shalom cannot exist. Shalom is not for the many, while a few suffer; nor is it for the few while many suffer. It must be available for everyone. In this way, shalom is everyone's concern. Shalom very much defines the common good. In this sense, shalom is also very close to Native American views, which are more communal than individualistic. The connection of the individual to the community and the individual to societal structure has been diminished in some modern Euro-western societies. This shift can be explained in many ways, but the correct exegesis of shalom still remains — shalom produces change for the good of all.

As a social construct, shalom is also dynamic. Shalom is not a utopian destination; it is a constant journey. One does not wait on shalom;

11. Brueggemann, *Peace,* 18.
12. Brueggemann, *Peace,* 19-20.

one actually sets about the task of shalom. In other words, people need to be going about the business of making shalom and living out shalom. This active, persistent effort takes place at every level, from personal relationships to societal and structural transformation. "The doing of righteousness and justice results in the building of viable community, that is, shalom, in which the oppressed and disenfranchised have dignity and power."[13] For Native Americans, finding harmony is also practical, and it is accomplished through direct involvement in ways such as intervention and ceremonies.

The transformational aspects of shalom are apparent in the divine model. In Scripture, God is active through creation, in personal relationships, in covenant relationships, in the incarnation of Jesus, and in redemption; consequently, shalom is reflected in all God's activity. Shalom, therefore, is not detached from the reality of everyday life in the world, nor is it in any sense superspiritual, utopian, or otherworldly; rather, it exemplifies how seriously God takes the world. Again, Brueggemann aids our understanding. It is well-being that exists in the very midst of threats — from sword and drought and wild animals. "It is well-being of a material, physical, historical kind, not idyllic 'pie in the sky,' but 'salvation' in the midst of trees and crops and enemies — in the very places where people always have to cope with anxiety, to struggle for survival, and to deal with temptation."[14] The emphasis here concerns the very practical aspects of the value of shalom in everyday life. Active and practical, shalom never avoids the realities of an imperfect world.

Facing Shalom

As mentioned earlier, shalom seen simply as "peace" is an anemic translation. In fact, sometimes shalom must come through the active creation of conflict. For example, where injustice exists, living out shalom dictates that the structure perpetuating the injustice be transformed. Where marginalization of the weak, the poor, the disempowered, the "ethnic other," is present, living out shalom demands that someone challenge the oppressive system and lift up those who are being oppressed, because oppression is sin. Wherever shalom is broken, sin is present; and it demands Christ's restora-

13. Brueggemann, *Peace*, 7.
14. Brueggemann, *Peace*, 15.

tion, particularly if it be found in those who bear Christ's name. As one writer puts it, "God is for shalom and, therefore, against sin. In fact, we may safely describe evil as any spoiling of shalom, whether physically (e.g., by disease), morally, spiritually, or otherwise."[15] Sin, in a very real sense, can be defined as the absence of shalom.

As a result of the practicality of shalom, sin is neither ignored nor relegated to the private, more personal areas of life. Shalom makers clearly need to be active in the world, influencing society toward the vision of the Trinitarian community on earth reflecting God's desire for everyone to dwell in shalom. Sin is brokenness and an alienating force that works against God's vision, but shalom does not assert unattainable utopian dreams without prescribing the means to a "peaceable kingdom" (Isa. 9:7; Rom. 14:17).

At this point the Native American understanding of balance and harmony can be helpful. Traditionally, Native Americans understood our role on earth as those who restore harmony in very practical ways. Our indigenous ceremonies often require not only symbolic acts but also practical restitution and full restoration. A vivid example of practical shalom making is the ancient Cherokee cementation ceremony, which occurred annually each fall. At that time anyone with a grievance against a fellow Cherokee was required to participate in the ceremony.

The basic components of the ceremony included a fire and prayers that were spoken by the holy person. Then the families and friends on each side of the riff would face each other with the lead persons (those with whom the division originated) at the head of the line. Each would give an account of the offense. Then the persons would go to the fire to pray for the strength to forgive. The two would then strip naked and exchange clothes. Following this action they spoke words of forgiveness and vowed never to bring the issue up again. The pipe was passed back and forth down the line for everyone to smoke. Finally, gifts were exchanged and a feast was prepared by both parties for the whole community. The result was both ceremonial and practical.

Making peace, shalom peace, also may be costly. For example, according to the practicality of living out shalom, the benefactors of colonial expansion would surely need to make restitution to those they robbed. In order to enjoy a society operating in shalom in America, everyone, espe-

---

15. Cornelius Plantinga Jr., *Not the Way It's Supposed to Be: A Breviary of Sin* (Grand Rapids: Eerdmans, 1995), 14.

cially Christians, will need to be educated to understand how shalom is directly related to ideas of restitution. As Edward Powers notes, "In the tribal period the word *shillem* (a close linguistic cousin of shalom) was used to denote requital or payment or compensation. The ancient Semitic tribes stressed the necessity of compensatory acts to make up for property loss, murder, or death in battle. This making up [of the loss] is a type of peace-making in that it attempts to restore the whole. Shillem restores shalom."[16]

The ramifications of restitution are incredible if we consider how much wrong has actually been done in the world by the colonial enterprise. Still, such a huge task should reveal the simple reality that shalom has been ignored, causing the world to be in such a mess. Only by practicing shalom can humanity restore the Creator's intentions for this fragmented world. Wherever relationships are fragmented, it is by living out shalom that they can be made whole.

Individualistic societies cause people to feel lonely and alienated, but shalom will bring authentic relationships and restore a sense of community. Greed and injustice marginalize and destroy people and the earth, but shalom restores dignity to everyone and everything. Shalom is the very concept needed in order to understand God and to make sense of the Christ who died for the world. When humans begin to understand shalom, God's power will begin working through them. Jesus, the shalom Christ who brings a shalom kingdom, is God's final answer to a broken and fragmented world. As Brueggemann so aptly states:

> Shalom is the end of coercion. Shalom is the end of fragmentation. Shalom is the freedom to rejoice. Shalom is the courage to live an integrated life in a community of coherence. These are not simply neat values to be added on. They are a massive protest against the central values by which our world operates. The world depends on coercion. The world depends on fragmented loyalties. The world as presently ordered depends on these very conditions against which the gospel protects and to which it provides alternatives.[17]

16. Edward A. Powers, *Signs of Shalom* (Philadelphia: Joint Educational Development United Church Press, 1973), 15.
17. Brueggemann, *Peace*, 51.

CHAPTER TWO

Jesus: From Kingdom to Community of Creation

A Ministry of Shalom

Jesus, properly understood as shalom, coming into the world from the shalom community of the Trinity, is the intention of God's once-and-for-all mission. That is, the mission of birthing and restoring shalom to the world is in Christ, by Christ, and for the honor of Christ. Jesus' announcement in Luke 4:16-27 is one of many references to his cosmic link to shalom-based spirituality. Strangely though, Luke situates what must be one of the most universally important announcements in the context of Nazareth, a small hamlet in the province of Galilee.

Nazareth was a strange choice for Jesus' inaugural address. After all, hadn't Jesus in approximately thirty years of wisdom keeping outgrown his small and insignificant hometown? Wouldn't a metropolitan center like Jerusalem, only three days' journey from Nazareth, or even nearby Tiberias be a better choice? Certainly his announcement would disseminate faster if given in a more populated and culturally important city. From the handful of references in the Scriptures, and according to the scant first-century historical references, Nazareth appears to be culturally inconsequential. Still, according to Luke, Jesus makes a seemingly calculated choice to be in his old hometown when it is time for the Isaiah 61 passage to be read in the synagogue. Why?

The reasons for Jesus' choice may have been mundane. Perhaps Nazareth was simply *en route,* or maybe he was testing small-town people's reactions (i.e., "if it plays in Scranton"), but according to the synoptic Gospel writers, Jesus had no affinity for large crowds or the "bright lights." Luke's record of Jesus' birthplace, as mentioned previously, implies that God does not seem to be impressed with human aptitude or great human achievements.

Perhaps Luke's most paradoxical expression of this principle is found in Acts 17:26-27, quoting the apostle Paul where he describes God's purpose of spreading humanity across the planet "so they might find God." According to most natural human reasoning, when you want someone to find something, you send them to one place, not across the whole planet. Paul chronicles a similar paradox in 1 Corinthians 1:20 when he says, "So where does this leave the philosophers, the scholars, and the world's brilliant debaters? God has made the wisdom of this world look foolish." The principle seems to defy much of the present worth of mass media advertising techniques or even what sells today as effective communication. It appears, according to Luke and several of the other Gospel writers, that when God wants all humanity to know something important, he invests his time and efforts in obscurity.

A less anthropocentric rationale for God's quirky communication style might understand that *all* of creation, not just human creation, is witness to God's truth. After all, human beings make up just a small part of life on earth. It seems that from the Almighty's purview, heaven and earth are the primary witnesses to God's pronouncements.[1] Could it be that, the farther removed from creation we become, or the more invested in the power of human ingenuity, the less we notice the importance of the things of God? The corollary is certainly true for Jesus' choice to reveal the importance of his earthly ministry in Nazareth.

Jesus stood up at the synagogue in his hometown and read the passage from Isaiah:

> The Spirit of the Sovereign LORD is upon me,
>   for the LORD has anointed me
>   to bring good news to the poor.
> He has sent me to comfort the brokenhearted
>   and to proclaim that captives will be released
>   and prisoners will be freed.
> He has sent me to tell those who mourn
>   that the time of the LORD's favor has come,

---

1. I.e., Deuteronomy 4:26; 30:19.

26

and with it, the day of God's anger against their enemies.
To all who mourn in Israel,
  he will give a crown of beauty for ashes,
a joyous blessing instead of mourning,
  festive praise instead of despair.
In their righteousness, they will be like great oaks
  that the LORD has planted for his own glory.

They will rebuild the ancient ruins,
  repairing cities destroyed long ago.
They will revive them,
  though they have been deserted for many generations.
Foreigners will be your servants.
  They will feed your flocks
and plow your fields
  and tend your vineyards.
You will be called priests of the LORD,
  ministers of our God.
You will feed on the treasures of the nations
  and boast in their riches.
Instead of shame and dishonor,
  you will enjoy a double share of honor
You will possess a double portion of prosperity in your land,
  and everlasting joy will be yours.

"For I, the LORD, love justice.
  I hate robbery and wrongdoing.
I will faithfully reward my people for their suffering
  and make an everlasting covenant with them.
Their descendants will be recognized
  and honored among the nations.
Everyone will realize that they are a people
  the LORD has blessed."

I am overwhelmed with joy in the LORD my God!
  For he has dressed me with the clothing of salvation
  and draped me in a robe of righteousness.
I am like a bridegroom in his wedding suit
  or a bride with her jewels.

The Sovereign LORD will show his justice to the nations
    of the world.
  Everyone will praise him!
His righteousness will be like a garden in early spring,
    with plants springing up everywhere. (Isa. 61 NLT)

What God appeared to be saying through the prophet Isaiah was familiar to those in the synagogue at Nazareth. Isaiah was describing how God will rescue the poor, heal broken hearts, bring good news to the oppressed, and free prisoners. It was already clear to the listening crowd that Isaiah was referring to the concept of *Jubilee*, "the acceptable year of the Lord" when those who have been marginalized will be restored to their rightful place of dignity. During Jubilee, security, honor, fecundity, justice, and blessing are also promised along with salvation. Many of those in ancient Israel understood the ramifications of the coming of a *Jubilee Year*.

Jubilee was the culmination of *the law of sevens*. In Scriptures such as Exodus chapter 16 (provision) and Leviticus chapter 25 (through the system of the law of sevens), Yahweh sets forth a way for Israel to ensure the principles of shalom were being observed. On every seventh day every person and every creature that toiled for a living were required to cease from their labor and rest. Following this course, a few of the images brought to mind are those of God resting on the seventh day of creation and also the provision of manna supplied by God in the wilderness.

In the first account of creation, embedded within the seventh day is the connection to all creation. When all creation is right, God ceases from his "labor" to enjoy it because human beings, who are rightly related to all creation, reflect the Creator's best intentions for our world (cf. Ps. 19:1). In the seventh-day Sabbath we find the injunction for all humanity, and also their working livestock, to cease laboring and enjoy the day by recognizing God's sacredness (holiness) and the sacredness of all creation. Shalom as it is intended to be lived involves the recognition that everything is sacred. On the seventh-day Sabbath, those who labor are called to reflect on the goodness and sacredness of the Creator and the creation.

Like God supplying the manna in the wilderness, on the Sabbath day humans were to provide food enough for themselves and their donkeys, oxen, horses, etcetera, prior to the actual day. On the Sabbath day the accomplishments of human ingenuity are put to rest and humans are called to remember that ultimately, everything we have comes from God. The remainder of creation seems to be able to recognize their reliance on God during the Sabbath and every other day for their needs (cf. Ps. 145:15-16; Luke 12:24). The exception for nondomesticated creatures may have been on the Sabbath when the Sabbath-keeping humans were not around to chase the critters away from their crops!

Another image of the Sabbath Day that comes to mind is one in which the servant or slave and foreigners among the Israelites were given that day to refresh themselves (Exod. 23:12). In this we see the antecedent of the Jubilee announcement in Isaiah 61 when the captives are fully released! The Exodus and Leviticus passages also describe a Sabbath Year.

> The LORD spoke to Moses on Mount Sinai, saying: "Speak to the people of Israel and say to them: When you enter the land that I am giving you, the land shall observe a sabbath for the LORD. For six years you shall sow your field, and for six years you shall prune your vineyard, and gather in their yield; but in the seventh year there shall be a sabbath of complete rest for the land, a sabbath for the LORD: you shall not sow your field or prune your vineyard. You shall not reap the aftergrowth of your harvest or gather the grapes of your unpruned vine: it shall be a year of complete rest for the land. You may eat what the land yields during its sabbath — you, your male and female slaves, your hired and your bound laborers who live with you; for your livestock also, and for the wild animals in your land all its yield shall be for food." (Lev. 25:1-7)

One purpose of the Sabbath year was to allow the land to rest and grow what it would naturally produce on its own without planting. On the Sabbath year no one was to work the land. On normal years a person's land was divided into seven sections. Each year one-seventh of the land was left unplanted so that it would rejuvenate and so the poor of the community could raise food for themselves. (Another provision for the poor was the command to leave the edges of the fields uncut so the poor could harvest something for themselves.) All of these injunctions were concerned about the well-being of the land; the poor; livestock and wild creatures; and the landowner, who seemed to require a higher learning curve than other creatures when it came to learning about trusting Yahweh for provision. Apparently, generosity and how to be a caretaker for creation in a reciprocating relationship was something that humans had to be required to practice on a regular basis in order to incorporate it into their lives.

But the Sabbath concept was not just a seventh day and a seventh year; it also came on every seventh set of seven years — and that year was called Jubilee! After forty-nine years (seven Sabbath years) came Jubilee, the culmination of and fulfillment of all God's Sabbath intentions. On every fiftieth year numerous actions were called for, but the following three principles are the main concern:

- All debts were canceled, so there would be no liabilities.
- All prisoners were set free.
- All land was redistributed by giving it back to those who originally possessed it.

Jubilee was good news for the poor. Sabbath, and especially Jubilee, was the awaited opportunity for new starts among marginalized people. The Acceptable Year of the Lord was the chance the oppressed needed in order to find new hope. Paradoxically, while the Year of Jubilee was good news to the poor, it might have felt like bad news to the rich and prosperous. Jubilee was good news to the oppressed but bad news to the oppressor. Certainly Mary, the mother of Jesus, understood the implications at the announcement of her pregnancy when she sang in Luke 1:51-53, "His mighty arm has done tremendous things! He has scattered the proud and haughty ones. He has brought down princes from their thrones and exalted the humble. He has filled the hungry with good things and sent the rich away with empty hands." Mary, and those during Jesus' time, understood well the radical implications of a Jubilee Year. Why were such radical social measures needed? The answer according to Isaiah 61 was because God "loves justice" and he "hates robbery and wrongdoing."

God's will and cosmic design is that no one suffer unjustly, but because human beings create unjust systems, shalom-type social parameters must serve as a social safety net to offset human disobedience. In order to create a shalom system of social harmony, no person could be oppressed for too long without hope of ease and eventual release; no family could remain in poverty for generations; no land could be worked until it was depleted and useless; no animals could go hungry for too long. Any of these violations of shalom that were left unmitigated for too long would upset the natural order of reciprocity fixed in all creation.

The Year of Jubilee ensured God's sense of justice for everyone, just in case justice was not being enacted by God's people in the way it was supposed to be done. Put in proper perspective, Sabbath days, Sabbath years, and Jubilee years were simply rehearsals for the real "game day," and in the understanding of Jesus, who had the final playbook, "game day" was to live out shalom every day.

Although it is difficult to disprove the negative, scholars have not been able to find a time in Israel's history when the Year of Jubilee was actually practiced. Unfortunately, that likely meant that upon hearing the injunction of Yahweh in Isaiah 61, the people would be inclined to interpret its meaning more as a moral injunction than a literal one. Some ancient Israelites may have understood it more metaphorically, as the announcement of a Messiah or a Messianic day when Yahweh would overthrow Israel's oppressors. In either case, Jesus' friends and family in Nazareth were not expecting him, as he read the Isaiah scroll that day, to push both literal and metaphorical understandings of Isaiah 61 past their comfortable limits and claim that he himself was the fulfillment of Jubilee, the Sabbath system, and ultimately shalom.

Jesus also had a different interpretation of ancient Israel's assumed privilege that surprised even his kin and neighbors. Words in the Isaiah 61 passage, like "Their descendants will be recognized and honored among the nations"; "Everyone will realize that they are a people the LORD has blessed"; and "The Sovereign LORD will show his justice to the nations of the world. Everyone will praise him," were generally interpreted by Israelites to mean that Israel would keep some divine advantage over all other nations. In other words, through their nationalistic myths, their stories of exceptionalism, it was obvious to many in ancient Israel that "God was on their side." It must have sounded strange when Jesus began reflecting on the Isaiah passage. The way Jesus interpreted what it meant for his own nation to be "chosen" was very different than many of his fellow Jews who were present.

In Luke's account (Luke 4:18ff.), Jesus reads Isaiah's prophecy and announces that "today, the scripture has been fulfilled!" At that point, there appears to be little reaction to Jesus' interpretation. Someone comments about his family, which in the broader picture means they may have been questioning his understanding of Jubilee (which, as I stated earlier, also included the Sabbath systems and the whole shalom concept). But Jesus doesn't expound on his announcement. Instead, Jesus continues tracking with the Isaiah passage in order to comment on their misinterpretation of God's favoring Israel over all other nations.

"But the truth is, there were many widows in Israel in the time of Elijah, when the heaven was shut up three years and six months, and there was a severe famine over all the land; yet Elijah was sent to none of them except to a widow at Zarephath in Sidon. There were also many lepers in Israel in the time of the prophet Elisha, and none of them was cleansed except Naaman the Syrian." When they heard this, all in the synagogue were filled with rage. (Luke 4:25-28)

The reaction to Jesus pointing out their ethnocentrism was downright hostile. In Jesus' understanding of God's plan, "chosen" did not translate as "better than." Jesus, unlike many of his fellow Israelites, was able to look at the same Scriptures and see Yahweh's involvement with those outside Israel. Jesus understood that the benefits of living out shalom were meant for everyone, not just Israel. Jesus recognized, not just a kingdom come for *his* people, but a community made up of *all* nations.

Kingdom and Community

Christ's clear call to the "kingdom" (in Greek, *Basileia tou Theou*) may be understood as a time and place where God is in charge, namely — shalom. Jesus' kingdom announcements reveal that his incarnation was the once-and-for-all divine intention and that God was still calling all people into shalom community. Jesus lived out a shalom life, pleasing to God, being led by the Holy Spirit and in communion with God. He was always inviting people, especially the marginalized, into God's community or kingdom. Jesus not only demonstrated shalom in his earthly lifetime, but he is the ultimate shalom come from God. Jesus' call to kingdom is most clearly recognized in context as a *shalom kingdom.*

According to Jesus, the kingdom, which may also be understood as a parallel concept for Jubilee, required a different way of living. "The time promised by God has come at last!" he announced. "The time is fulfilled, and the kingdom of God has come near; repent, and believe in the good news" (Mark 1:15). The alternative way of living that Jesus taught, and lived out, and to which he called others to turn toward, was completely consistent with shalom.

Jesus' use of the term "kingdom" was never intended to be understood as an unrelated concept to what had been previously taught by the prophets and what was found in other Scriptures. Jesus said, until now "John the Baptist, the law of Moses and the messages of the prophets were your guides. But now the Good News of the Kingdom of God is preached, and everyone is eager to get in" (Luke 16:16 NLT). Jesus didn't destroy the former message of his predecessors. His emphasis was on the fulfillment of the best promises of the old system, and since Jubilee had probably never been practiced in ancient Israel, it was actually something new.

According to the synoptic Gospel writers, Jesus spent a great deal of effort trying to bring the Pharisees into a new way of thinking about God's shalom way of living that he called the "kingdom." Jesus' made direct statements to the Pharisees, apparently trying to get them to join in his understanding of how the former system relates to the new. "And he said to them, 'Therefore every scribe who has been trained for the kingdom of heaven is like the master of a household who brings out of his treasure what is new and what is old'" (Matt. 13:52).

Jesus' great problem with the Pharisees was their reluctance to accept his new understanding of a shalom kingdom. In this effort we find Jesus trying to build a bridge between the priestly and prophetic divide of ancient Israel. Jesus understood the best intentions of the Leviticus and Sabbath codes. He did not ignore them. In his frustration with the Pharisees we can see how the priestly and prophetic realms merge and integrate into praxis. Jesus demonstrates to the religious leaders of his day how a narrow interpretation of the priestly codes can become dangerous, being far from God's original intentions. In Luke 11:52 (NLT) Jesus says, "What sorrow awaits you experts in religious law! For you remove the key to knowledge from the people. You don't enter the Kingdom yourselves, and you prevent others from entering."

Jesus told several parables to the Pharisees directly relating to their missing the point. For example, the story of the workers who felt treated unfairly ends with the conclusion: "But he replied to one of them, 'Friend, I am doing you no wrong; did you not agree with me for the usual daily wage? Take what belongs to you and go; I choose to give to this last the same as I give to you. Am I not allowed to do what I choose with what belongs to me? Or are you envious because I am generous?' So the last will be first, and the first will be last" (Matt. 20:13-16 NLT; see also Matt. 21:33-43; 22:1-14). In this parable Jesus was addressing the Pharisees' and teachers' jealousy over those who have not kept the letter of the priestly requirements. The message of a shalom kingdom is that everyone is eligible for entrance. The shalom kingdom is always inviting others, especially the disempowered and marginalized, and is thus ever expanding.

Jesus' invitation is clear; keeping the strict injunctions of the Levitical codes and ritual requirements is not a means of privilege in God's eyes. They were meant to be a form of training. At the same time, the prophetic tradition summoned the fairest expectations of justice among people. In Jesus' way of thinking, being chosen was simply responding to God's generous offer; it bore no rank or privilege. In fact, reliance on such human achievements runs contrary to shalom living. Adherence to the Law, as a means of justification, could even keep a person out of God's kingdom. In the middle of Matthew's recording of Jesus' parables to the Pharisees, Jesus clearly and directly interprets his point:

> Then Jesus explained his meaning: "I tell you the truth, corrupt tax collectors and prostitutes will get into the Kingdom of God before you do. For John the Baptist came and showed you the right way to live, but you didn't believe him, while tax collectors and prostitutes did. And even when you saw this happening, you refused to believe him and repent of your sins." (Matt. 21:31b-32 NLT)

Ancient Shalom and the New Kingdom Meet in John

Why was Jesus so impressed with John the Baptist? (Hint: It probably wasn't because of his coarse camel-hair clothing or his bug diet.) Jesus saw in John a proper understanding of shalom. John's message and lifestyle were the visual object lesson upon which Jesus relied to help him interpret the meaning of God's shalom kingdom. John cared about justice and the marginalized, not about his own advancement. The Baptist preached repentance of anything contrary to Jubilee's promises. Jesus said that John "showed you the right way to live." John the Baptist understood some segments of ancient Israel's nationalistic pride and ethnocentric arrogance and he knew it had no place in God's shalom kingdom. "Do not presume to say to yourselves, 'We have Abraham as our ancestor'; for I tell you, God is able from these stones to raise up children to Abraham. Even now the axe is lying at the root of the trees; every tree therefore that does not bear good fruit is cut down and thrown into the fire" (Matt. 3:9-10).

When asked by the crowds how to live in the way God wants them to live, John answers succinctly, pointing out shalom actions that consist of justice and care for the poor:

> In reply he said to them, "Whoever has two coats must share with anyone who has none; and whoever has food must do likewise." Even tax-

collectors came to be baptized, and they asked him, "Teacher, what should we do?" He said to them, "Collect no more than the amount prescribed for you." Soldiers also asked him, "And we, what should we do?" He said to them, "Do not extort money from anyone by threats or false accusation, and be satisfied with your wages." (Luke 3:11-14)

John was clear in his message that shalom had been neglected and now needed to be reinstated. Jesus' example to the Pharisees was no less direct, but he did have a more contextual approach. When understood in context, one of Jesus' most beloved parables, the parable of the Prodigal Son — or, as I call it, the story of Two Lost Sons — is an injunction to the Pharisees and religious teachers to recognize and begin to participate in the correct understanding of the shalom kingdom of God.

Jesus' story, which I will deal with in full in the final chapter, begins with the context of those leaders complaining about his association with the ritually and morally unclean. In each of the three parables — the lost sheep, the lost coin, and the lost sons — Jesus portrays the kingdom as a community of restoration and celebration. In the final story, Luke ends the parable with the oldest son (who represents the Pharisees, the religious teachers, and by proxy their emphasis on a narrow priestly understanding of the holiness codes) standing outside the party while the father, who was feeding the whole community, including servants and the poor, entreats him to come in.

Birds and Flowers

Many other sayings of Jesus concerning the kingdom can be attributed to the fulfillment of his understanding of shalom, including Matthew 19:24, where Jesus tells the rich ruler to sell his riches and give them to the poor. In doing so, Jesus points out that rich people will find it nearly impossible to enter the kingdom (cf. Mark 10:23). In Matthew's Gospel, Jesus concludes the lesson by pointing out that in order to live out the way God desires for his followers means they will share in everything, including homes, relationships, and property. Living out a truly shalom life in the kingdom is God's answer to living in abundance. To share wealth, as opposed to privately hoarding wealth (vv. 29-31), is truly abundant living. Sharing wealth is the standard expectation of all those who desire to live out shalom.

In Matthew 6:22-34, Jesus addresses wealth and worry by widening the circle of the kingdom to the most obvious concept, that of creation itself.

> "The eye is the lamp of the body. So, if your eye is healthy, your whole body will be full of light; but if your eye is unhealthy, your whole body will be full of darkness. If then the light in you is darkness, how great is the darkness! No one can serve two masters; for a slave will either hate the one and love the other, or be devoted to the one and despise the other. You cannot serve God and wealth.
>
> "Therefore I tell you, do not worry about your life, what you will eat or what you will drink, or about your body, what you will wear. Is not life more than food, and the body more than clothing? Look at the birds of the air; they neither sow nor reap nor gather into barns, and yet your heavenly Father feeds them. Are you not of more value than they? And can any of you by worrying add a single hour to your span of life? And why do you worry about clothing? Consider the lilies of the field, how they grow; they neither toil nor spin, yet I tell you, even Solomon in all his glory was not clothed like one of these. But if God so clothes the grass of the field, which is alive today and tomorrow is thrown into the oven, will he not much more clothe you — you of little faith? Therefore do not worry, saying, 'What will we eat?' or 'What will we drink?' or 'What will we wear?' For it is the Gentiles who strive for all these things; and indeed your heavenly Father knows that you need all these things. But strive first for the kingdom of God and his righteousness, and all these things will be given to you as well. So do not worry about tomorrow, for tomorrow will bring worries of its own. Today's trouble is enough for today."

In Jesus' understanding, God's ways are set. There can be no divided loyalties. The new way of kingdom living is about the consistency of living out the fulfillment of the ancient Sabbath and Jubilee systems. It even dates all the way back to the story of creation in the garden of Eden. Living out shalom means taking into account all of creation in reciprocal relationships and learning from creation as object lessons for understanding God's shalom provision. In shalom, one fills Heaven's purse by redistributing wealth on earth to all who are in need. In the shalom intention of the created order, God takes care of creation through people living out shalom. The promises of shalom are for the whole of creation. Human beings play a role in seeing that the order is maintained.

Even the ancient covenants, whether explicit or implied, are never just meant to be between Israel and Yahweh, or even just between all humanity and God. Whether the rest of creation is omitted because the covenants are viewed too narrowly through Israel's nationalistic lens, or through the lens of a dualistic western worldview, the Creator is still concerned with all of creation. God's injunction to all creation, not just humans, is to "be fruitful and multiply." Later, in his covenant with Noah and his descendants (Gen. 9:10), we see that God has also included "all living creatures" in the covenant. Another instance of the covenant language actually including other, nonhuman creation is Hosea 2:18: "I will make for you a covenant on that day with the wild animals, the birds of the air, and the creeping things of the ground; and I will abolish the bow, the sword, and war from the land; and I will make you lie down in safety."

God's concern on earth for a shalom kingdom is for all his creation. The writer of Proverbs 9:10 equates care for animals with righteousness: "The godly care for their animals, but the wicked are always cruel." Isaiah 40:26 tells us that God calls the stars by name. Notice how the psalmist points out the relationship between God's love for all creation, creation's testimony of God, and the relationship between all creation and shalom in Psalm 145:9-19.

> The LORD is good to all,
> and his compassion is over all that he has made.
> All your works shall give thanks to you, O LORD,
> and all your faithful shall bless you.
> They shall speak of the glory of your kingdom,
> and tell of your power,
> to make known to all people your mighty deeds,
> and the glorious splendor of your kingdom.
> Your kingdom is an everlasting kingdom,
> and your dominion endures throughout all generations.
> The LORD is faithful in all his words,
> and gracious in all his deeds.
> The LORD upholds all who are falling,
> and raises up all who are bowed down.
> The eyes of all look to you,
> and you give them their food in due season.
> You open your hand,
> satisfying the desire of every living thing.

The LORD is just in all his ways,
and kind in all his doings.
The LORD is near to all who call on him,
to all who call on him in truth.
He fulfils the desire of all who fear him;
he also hears their cry, and saves them.

In the psalm, God's promise follows the testimony of creation. The fallen and those bent beneath their loads may be referring to livestock such as donkeys and oxen, who receive their food "in due season." While not excluding humans from the psalm, I think it is logical, given the context, that it is the eyes of those beasts of burden who look to God in hope, to supply their needs. Even God's righteousness is measured in his provision (v. 16). God supplies "every living thing." Such descriptions cause the reader to be reminiscent of God's provision in other scriptural places such as the garden of Eden, in the wilderness, and in Jesus' statement that God even sustains the flowers in the field and the birds of the air.

Metaphors of the Kingdom

There is a symbiotic connection between the ancient Hebrew concepts of Sabbath, Jubilee, and shalom. This synthesis comes together most clearly in Jesus. Jesus suggests that a new way to live on a daily basis be called the "kingdom." Using the context of Roman occupation and its imperial order, Jesus contextualized the shalom concept to be understood in his day as the kingdom or reign of God. In doing so, he did not exclude the greater understanding that all of creation is participating in this kingdom. Given his understanding of the above passages, and others like them, it was clear that Jesus understood and taught that the kingdom includes all of creation.

I believe Jesus' intention to use the metaphor of a "kingdom" was primarily because it was a forceful concept in the context of empire. Though the term "kingdom" was appropriate at the time, the military reference should not lead us to forget that the kingdom Jesus referred to was Jubilee contextualized, and it was energized by its setting in the midst of imperial oppression.[2] Unfortunately, the imperial idea of the "kingdom" as a milita-

2. There may be a case to be made that Jesus used the term "kingdom" in reference to

rized realm is typically how Christians still continue using it after two millennia. Jesus' numerous parables and encounters demonstrate how he also used other language that lent itself to a more natural and communal imagery that was also plain to his hearers, i.e., seeds, trees, birds, vineyards. Today, it is perplexing to me that Christians still insist on using the word "kingdom" with the same meaning and force as they use the term "crusade" for an evangelistic outreach.

May I suggest that maintaining the imperial metaphor has not served Christianity well? I would like to see us move from a first-century military framework, of "king" and "kingdom" (with which Americans have no lived experience), to our present context of global awareness, pluralism, and holism. Given our history and the age in which we now live, new metaphors may help us find a better path in following Christ. I suggest that the greater context for primary consideration might be "Community of Creation." A wider theological vision for the biblical kingdom construct makes more sense and has a more consistent application when understood as the community of creation.

We might begin to experiment with the phrase as an alterNative to the translation of Jesus' words, "the kingdom of God" and the "kingdom of Heaven."[3] The theological understanding of the community of creation is much broader than simply being a replacement phrase for "the kingdom of God" or "kingdom of Heaven" and, as I have argued, it may even be closer to the meaning understood by Jesus and his local contemporaries than the popular military connotation. This understanding is also crucial, in contemporary Christianity, for making the connection between who Christ is as Creator, and the role he plays in the shalom construct in a whole new community living out God's shalom purposes on earth.

Christ is not just King, but Creator. Kings come and go, but the Creator is eternal. When we begin to recognize the cosmic implications of Christ as Creator, temporal concepts like governments, kingdoms, and rulers fade in comparison. In the next chapter I will explore in more detail what seemed to be implicitly known among many of the writers of the New Testament, and perhaps those in the early church — namely, that Jesus of Nazareth is not just a representative of God but God himself; and, that Jesus' efficacy in creation was primary and central to the human story.

Israel's need for a true king. I am not convinced that Jesus would go down that path, because God never intended Israel to have a king.

3. "Heaven" is used in Matthew's Gospel to avoid saying the name of God.

As the writers of the New Testament reflected on the consequences of such a great possibility, they began to understand that cosmic empires trump their ideas of earthly kingdoms that are made heavenly.

In our day, empire is affecting the whole planet in a very destructive way. Perhaps "community of creation" can be understood not just as a theological construct, but an alternate phrase encompassing Jesus' meaning in our global context while still retaining its original anti-imperialist nuances. The phrase "community of creation" is specifically infused with biblical and indigenous meaning because it assumes all of creation is participating in the new community, not just humans. A broader, contextualized phrase such as "community of creation" may help to move western Christians from provincialism to a point where they understand that embedded within Jesus' indigenous teachings of the community of creation is a key, not just for saving us, but also for healing our planet.

> For God in all his fullness
>   was pleased to live in Christ,
> and through him God reconciled
>   everything to himself.
> He made [shalom] with everything in heaven and on earth
> by means of Christ's blood on the cross. (Col. 1:19-20 NLT)

Jesus Christ is our Sabbath rest. Christ is our shalom. His community of creation is the logic of manna. Jesus is the daily and eternal fulfillment to the Year of Jubilee. Justice and equality, provision and freedom, salvation and healing of all creation are found in Christ. As those who have answered the call to represent Christ by living in the community of creation, Christians, above everyone else, must realize that Jesus' shalom community will only manifest itself wherever we act in accordance with shalom. As Jesus' shalom-keepers we are to exhibit a new order — a Sabbath way, a Jubilee lifestyle, and a shalom way of being in, with, and for the community of creation.

CHAPTER THREE

God's First Discourse: Connected to Creation

Creation Is Really Good!

"Then God looked over all he had made, and he saw that it was very good!" (Gen. 1:31a NLT). In the account of creation found in Genesis chapter 1, we see that God created everything, and everything God created is described in Hebrew not just as good, but as "really good!" The writer of the Genesis passage gives us the sense that the Creator is very excited about creation. I imagine it is similar to how an artist feels after that once-in-a-lifetime song, painting, or sculpture perfectly comes together and feels complete in every sense. It should comfort us to know that the Creator has such strong feelings about the creation.

When God says all creation is good, this judgment is not a light opinion about the state of creation; it is a royal decree. In the pronouncement that "it is good," the Creator is making an accurate judgment about all that exists. By proclaiming that everything is good, right, in order, and as it should be, God sets the state of earthly normalcy. "Good" becomes the once-and-for-all standard of life on earth. What I particularly like in the first Genesis account of creation is that the writer shows us the Creator's finesse.

Unhurried, the Spirit "hovers," and then, at just the right time, he intentionally begins to work through each color on his palette, including the celestial water, space, and sky. Then God creates the terrestrial waters and the earth, including the plants, trees, and fruits. Next, God watches the seeds from those plants bear after their own kind. Subsequently, the Creator sets the celestial and the terrestrial in rhythm together, including the balances of night and day, summer, fall, winter, and spring. The rhythm turns months into years. Then God fills the waters with fish and the skies with birds, and they all increase.

Whales come together in pods in the Puget Sound. Porpoises travel in schools throughout the Caribbean. Salmon make their first runs up the rivers of Scotland. Flamingos land in voluminous flocks on Lake Tanganyika in East Africa's Great Rift Valley. Canada geese make their first Vs as they repeatedly cross America's Central Flyway. The waters teem with fish. The birds dot the skies. Then, animals of every form, stripe, and color appear, and finally, human beings are created. The writer gives us the sense in this account that the Creator immensely enjoyed creating our world. The act of creation was not impetuous or hasty but instead was deliberate and thoughtful, stretching out over time, as if it was all done so the Creator could receive maximum pleasure.

In the first account of creation, each action and each result of God's action is differentiated. Not one created part *is* the other, nor does it *become* the other. Each part of creation was made unique and after its own kind, special. And yet, each part is incomplete without the whole, and everything is being and becoming in relationship to and with the other. The writer of this creation account has given us a record of the most beautiful dance ever danced, the most engaging song ever sung, the most intimate sculpture ever made; and yet it is so much more than any one of these. It is the essence of harmony and balance.

The celestials regulate the balance of the terrestrials. The night dusk comes to softly compel all creation to enter into rest and the calm brings about refreshing coolness to the world. The advent of the day provides new life and new opportunities like the embrace of warmth for plants, animals, and humans. The moon regulates all the waters. The sun regulates each season. The seasons regulate all creation on the earth and in the sky as annual activities; bears hibernate, and birds migrate, and people store wood and food for the winter and plant seeds in the spring. Everything created is in harmony and balance with everything else and with the Creator. The first week of creation is a grand picture of shalom on the earth.

From God's purview there is an interconnectedness of all God has made. All things are designed and created beautifully by their Creator. Each part of the created whole bears the mark of its Creator. Each element works in relationship with all the others. Each ingredient is connected through its common origin and, together, all share a common location in the universe; and when God is finished with creation there is a pause on the seventh day. Not a pause as if to look back and second-guess, but an intentional pause to celebrate the way it is. The Aboriginal Rainbow Elders in Australia say the Creator sang on the seventh day. The meaning is like that of a gathering or a community "get-together" where celebration is the only priority. The celebration is a party because everything is harmonious as it was meant to be. This is God's shalom creation party. Though told in slightly different ways, many indigenous peoples around the world are able to recognize this story, and this pause, as the Harmony Way.

In first-century Judea, the apostle Paul also recognizes the universality of the creation story and uses it as a backdrop for how Christ brings all things together in harmony. Paul borrows the energy from the idea of the artful exuberance God has for creation when referencing the reconciliation of Jews and Gentiles in Ephesians 2:10: "For we are God's masterpiece. He has created us anew in Christ Jesus, so we can do the good things he planned for us long ago."

In Ephesians chapter 2 the apostle seems to understand something about humanity "mirroring" the good works of creation with our own good works. According to Paul, we, as humans, are participants in the continuation of creation by manifesting good in our world. As we do good in Christ, harmony is restored, or as Paul calls it, "reconciliation." The culmination of the reconciliation process that Paul references is shalom (v. 14).

I think that in Paul's mind the idea of God's shalom is not divorced from creation, but as we can plainly see from the earliest Genesis account, creation is central to our understanding of shalom. Creation (what God did and continues to do daily) and the carrying out of shalom (what we are to do daily) are inextricably interwoven. We have the opportunity each day to participate in God's shalom activities. Among Native Americans, many tribes have a word or several words describing this same ancient Hebrew shalom reality. We may refer to the comprehension of and the commonalities of an ancient understanding of shalom simply as the Harmony Way.

Jesus as the Shalom Restorer of Justice and Dignity

That night there were shepherds staying in the fields nearby, guarding their flocks of sheep. Suddenly, an angel of the Lord appeared among them, and the radiance of the Lord's glory surrounded them. . . . Suddenly, the angel was joined by a vast host of others — the armies of heaven — praising God and saying, "Glory to God in highest heaven, and [shalom] on earth to those with whom God is pleased." (Luke 2:8-14)

The Creator has never abandoned these wonderful plans for the Harmony Way on earth. God certainly never intended shalom to be merely an after-earth reality! The Harmony Way is embedded in the created order and is meant to be lived out *on* earth by all creation. The Harmony Way, or shalom, is revealed deeply in Jesus' life, even as a baby, with many of God's creatures surrounding him at his entrance into the world.

Think about the reality of the story for a moment. With "no room in the inn," the stables must have been pretty full. I have never farmed camels, but I have years of experience with horses, cows, sheep, goats, and chickens. The fact is, when crowded into a barn (or a cave) not only do all these animals not get along well, but they stink! And their stink together is not like the smell of a stew where all flavors blend to create a nice aroma. "Livestock Manure Stew" smells much worse than any one of them smells by itself. Now add humans to the mix! Not really a pleasant thought, eh? Please continue with me just a bit longer.

In the midst of this crowded, stinky place is a feed trough. Deep under the hay, as a result of all the animals' noses constantly milling around, is where most of the grains have sifted to and piled up. The smarter animals (likely the goats and camels) move through the mulled-over hay and "mouth" their way to the bottom of the manger to find the grains. Exuding saliva, "sneeze juice," and snot from their nostrils, the animals continue to dip their face toward the protein-rich grain like kids bobbing for apples. It is in this kind of a place where Jesus is born. The Creator becomes a helpless child and is born in a barn and placed in the feed trough. I wonder if Christ had expected such a throne when he created the world? Likely so, for God's purposes are often so simple and obvious that we humans blunder all around them without ever recognizing them.

But modern humans may have the wrong idea about the birthplace of Jesus. The reality of the situation is that the Christ-child is born among those whom human beings regard the least. Pastoral people do value their animals, but they are still animals. Simple beasts of burden and future table food would never be thought of as central in a story of the Creator's birth, or would they? Perhaps there was something about the Harmony Way that the beasts of burden, the domestic livestock, the doves and mice, fleas and flies, etcetera understood, since they become the first audience to the most

44

visible demonstration of God's restoring life on earth back to the Creator's original intentions.

In Luke's account, after he grants domestic animals front-row seating, the lowly shepherds appear next on the invited guest list. While shepherd imagery was used in the Hebrew Testament to show God's care for God's people, it had lost much of its immediacy by the first century, especially around urban centers such as Jerusalem. Shepherding was among the occupations whose testimony was not allowed in a court of law,[1] and that is why the Creator saw fit for shepherds to be the first humans to receive the news of Christ's birth. It was only fitting for the announcement of the restoration of shalom on earth to be made to those whom society deemed untrustworthy. In such an act, the justice of shalom restores the dignity of the shepherds. But why were the shepherds degraded to such a low state in the first place?

Though I am making a calculated guess, I think I may have an answer. My answer came to me only after years of self-decolonization, but any colonized group might have come up with a similar understanding. My guess is that after years of struggling in court over ancient land rights that were being trampled by urban development, the wealthy developers, and those who had invested in the urban growth system, won their rights unjustly over the seemingly insignificant shepherds. The easiest path to secure such illegitimate rights was to prevent shepherds from testifying in court altogether. This pattern is all too familiar among indigenous people who face colonization and so-called development. A similar course of action was pursued by the Euro-Americans for centuries, beginning with John Winthrop and the earliest Pilgrims who annulled any Native claims to the land by declaring Indian rights illegal. "The Indians," he said, "had not 'subdued' the land, and therefore had only a 'natural' right to it, but not a 'civil right.' A 'natural right' did not have legal standing."[2]

Regardless of the reason for such unjust laws, for a time in the Creator's court, the shepherds were given exclusive rights to witness an event that even kings were prevented from seeing. The shepherds' testimony is valuable to the gospel story. The restoration of their dignity becomes central to God's Harmony Way purposes on earth because shalom always re-

---

1. See Joachim Jeremias, *Rediscovering the Parables: A Landmark Work in New Testament Interpretation* (New York: Charles Scribner's Sons, 1966).

2. Howard Zinn, *A People's History of the United States: 1492–Present* (New York: HarperCollins, 2003), 13-14.

stores dignity to the most marginalized of society. Depending on which Gospel account we read, other characters were also present at the birth of Jesus.

The Wise Men, who were Gentiles, were invited to partake in God's special Harmony Way event. Seen by many Jews as unworthy, these famous Gentiles' pilgrimage may have been recorded in order to convey a strong message to the "chosen" of Israel that everyone, from every nation (including the animal nations), is chosen and loved by God. The foundational principle of the community of creation is reaffirmed over and again by Jesus during his ministry, even to the disdain of his own village (see Luke 4:17ff.).[3] Furthermore, God has always accepted the Gentiles. The Hebrew Scriptures attest to the idea that each nation has its own relationship with the Creator; for example, in Amos 9:7 we read, "'Are you Israelites more important to me than the Ethiopians?' asks the Lord. 'I brought Israel out of Egypt, but I also brought the Philistines from Crete and led the Arameans out of Kir'" (NLT).

Clearly, in Jesus is found the message that living out shalom means that no one person, occupation, or nation is more important to God than another. Understanding the shalom of God in Christ means that the God of Israel is actively involved in the care for, and the plight of, all other peoples. Jesus understood his shalom ministry on earth in this universal light and as a result of this understanding, he most often "hung" with tax gatherers, women of all sorts, the untouchables, and sometimes Gentiles. Even Matthew's birth narrative of Jesus' paternal lineage includes women (a

---

3. The usual argument for the temporary exclusion of Gentiles from Jesus' ministry includes the direct statement Jesus makes while dealing with the Canaanite woman whose daughter needed healing, by responding to her that he was "sent only to the lost sheep of Israel" (Matt. 15:22-28). If we ignore the irony with which Jesus often spoke during such occasions, we might miss the juxtaposition of Jesus' response with that of his disciples, who preferred that she be sent away. Jesus' pattern of accepting women, Gentiles, and others while others urge him to reject them is clear throughout his ministry. Often Jesus' dialogical bantering comes with his initial resistance but culminates with the person obtaining his or her request. To understand Jesus' ministry in a light contrary to the inclusion of the Gentiles is inconsistent with his numerous dialogical forays that always resulted in his acceptance of lepers, beggars, prostitutes, Samaritans, and Gentiles. An anemic understanding of Jesus' attempt to put off the Canaanite woman in Matthew 15 would be particularly troubling in Matthew, given that the writer begins Jesus' lineage with "an introductory genealogy that includes four foreign women, and the conclusion provides mission discourse that contemplates disciples from any nation." Mark Brett, *Decolonizing God: The Bible in the Tides of Empire* (Sheffield, U.K.: Phoenix Press, 2008), 144.

widow and a prostitute) who are from foreign nations (Matt. 1:5). By the end of his life, the very story of Jesus' resurrection would depend on the testimony of women, another part of Judean society whose word was not trusted in the legal system.

Indeed, it was women who were given the power from the Creator to create life, including the life of Jesus, the Christ-child from Mary. Mary, the virgin, brought forth life in the same way the first human is brought forth from the virgin soil. This act is nothing new. In many of our indigenous stories Mother Earth brings forth humans and the Creator breathes life into them. In the Jewish-Christian continuance, mother Mary brings forth the Second Adam with the life-seed of the Creator. The restoration of the dignity of women is a central theme in a shalom trajectory. Jesus drew women around himself in order for them to understand that they too had the privilege and responsibility to become disciples, teachers, prophets, and apostles in God's shalom way. And it was women who would eventually have the honor to be the first to bring the testimony of Jesus' resurrection from the tomb. Without the restoration of the central role of women, there could have been no virgin birth. Without women, there could be no creation.

Intimate, Animate, and Sacred

Jesus' birth, and his whole life, was connected to all aspects of creation, from the animals in the stable, to the wheat in the field, to the grapes and figs in the vineyard, to the marginalized people of society. His worldview was one that understood the earth to be sacred. As my friend Bo Sanders reminded me once, the stories told by Jesus are primarily about creation. Jesus spoke primarily of birds, crops, fields, fruit, fish, water, light, trees, livestock, relationships, and so on. His worldview was *creation-centered* and not particularly mechanistic. Jesus, as a carpenter, could have just as easily spent his time reflecting on the importance of a mechanistic worldview by sharing stories referring primarily to wheels, chariots, shields, how mills operate, how the legal system operates, and so on. Our record indicates that Jesus spoke from and of the world to which he related best, that of creation — the world he himself formed.

In the western world we must remind ourselves that the Scriptures are written from a worldview that does not easily categorize creation into animate and inanimate realities. To Jesus, all of creation was alive. Jesus felt comfortable in relating to, and conversing with, what the western mind often calls inanimate. Jesus finds himself in situations that most Euro-western people would summarily discount. Jesus locates schools of fish and donkeys when needed; he borrows a coin from the mouth of a fish; he speaks to storms; he walks on water; he curses trees; and so on. And notice, the narratives do not suggest that anyone judges him a witch or something worse because of his view of creation.[4] The people around Jesus shared a similar worldview. Jesus, like so many in his day, was comfortable in a constant conversation with natural creation. He was not estranged from creation in the way most of us in the western world are today. By and large, moderns no longer live in close contact with the natural world or make their livings through dependency upon creation. Dependence on the comforts of modernity has caused us to drop the once-natural connection to creation.

Once upon a time in America, fishermen knew how to read the skies; sailors navigated by the stars; crops were planted and harvested according to the moon and upon naturally calculated estimations of rain and sun. In the modern world only the local weather person now makes his or her living based upon predicting nature. Most of us live insulated from the conversation with creation that Jesus and many of the biblical writers held daily.

Jesus, though he showed respect for Jerusalem, considered the whole created world to be sacred. According to Jesus, creation was considered so sacred that it was not to be demeaned by using it in an oath. Consider Matthew 5:34b-35a, for example, where he references the sacred earth: "Do not say, 'By heaven!' because heaven is God's throne. And do not say, 'By the earth!' because the earth is his footstool."[5] Other accounts, throughout the Psalms, Wisdom literature, and such, reveal the sacredness and the value of the creation to the Creator and to humans. Consider just two out of hundreds of examples. Here is the first:

> Go to the ant, you lazybones;
> consider its ways, and be wise.
> Without having any chief

---

4. The Pharisees called Jesus demon possessed because of his view of God, not because of his view of creation.

5. Granted, the context in this excerpt is to not just say you will do something but to actually do what you say you will do. Still, one would have a difficult time arguing that Jesus did not consider the heavens and the earth sacred after examining such a statement.

or officer or ruler,
it prepares its food in summer,
and gathers its sustenance in harvest.
How long will you lie there, O lazybones?
When will you rise from your sleep?
A little sleep, a little slumber,
a little folding of the hands to rest,
and poverty will come upon you like a robber,
and want, like an armed warrior. (Prov. 6:6-11)

The ants appears to be a continual source of inspiration, modeling for us how we should govern ourselves and manage our lives concerning our economic activities. This example also reveals an important aspect of sha-lom. The point should not be overlooked concerning how closely the principles of this short proverb align with the whole Sabbath system as shown in Leviticus 25. As I mentioned in chapter one, on the Sabbath day every person, ox, donkey, horse, and such, is to rest. All necessary labor is to be accomplished prior to the Sabbath so that people are free to rest. The seventh year was also to be observed as a year of Sabbath. Israel was to divide the land into seven sections. Each year one section of land was to be left to rejuvenate, and edges of fields were to be left for the poor to glean. Sowing and reaping crops were forbidden in the seventh year, so the poor and the animals could eat. It was a year of rest for the land. This meant a more disciplined and intentional approach to planning. Poor planning for a day might result in temporary hunger from a missed meal. Poor planning for a year could be disastrous for the planter and for the extreme poor who, through their dependency, would ultimately benefit from the planter's labor. The example of the ants shows humans how to trust the provisions of God. The ants store up for a time when they cannot work; Sabbath requires similar trust.

Another example of the sacred value of creation is found in Job 12:7-10. This amplified version draws us into a clear understanding of this passage.

For ask now the animals, and they will teach you [that God does not deal with His creatures according to their character]; ask the birds of the air, and they will tell you; or speak to the earth [with its other forms of life], and it will teach you; and the fish of the sea will declare [this truth] to you. Who [is so blind as] not to recognize in all these [that good and evil are promiscuously scattered throughout nature and human life] that it is God's hand which does it [and God's way]? In His hand is the life of every living thing and the breath of all mankind.

In this passage Job is admonishing one of his accusers to:

- talk to animals and then be taught from them
- talk to and listen to birds
- talk to the earth and other creation and expect to be taught from them
- listen to fish attest to the truth
- and, if you can't recognize God's hand in all creation, the implication is that you are blind!

These kinds of images can be disturbing to Euro-western minds that insist on assigning concepts like *inanimate* to living creation.[6] If a person's worldview negates them from being intimately connected in a reciprocal relationship to creation, the words of Job may appear foolish. And yet, there is nothing that seems inanimate about anything Job mentions. To Job, the animals, birds, fish, and the earth are all alive. So often people jump to accusations of animism or anthropomorphism when these kinds of scriptures are discussed, but according to the Scriptures, not only are the animals made from the same earthly clay as humans, but the same sacred breath in humans also resides in creation.[7]

If we try to read the Scriptures through the worldview of the biblical authors, Euro-western categories may be inadequate in helping to understand humanity's relationships to creation. Modern Euro-western categories most often have human beings over and above the rest of creation. Several scriptures should give us pause to rethink the way we view our own human superiority.

I also said to myself, "As for humans, God tests them so that they may see that they are like the animals. Surely the fate of human beings is like that of the animals; the same fate awaits them both: As one dies, so

6. Some languages assign gender in speech to categories while many others assign animacy. Assigning animacy goes much deeper than linguistic taxonomic structure. Some languages, like the Cherokee language, divide animacy between animals and plants but still contain ceremonies requiring the adherent to address the plants in speech. Cherokees also retain stories in which plants are speaking, making decisions, having feelings, etc.

7. Genesis 1:30; 7:15; Psalm 33:6; 150:6.

dies the other. All have the same breath; humans have no advantage over animals. Everything is meaningless. All go to the same place; all come from dust, and to dust all return." (Eccles. 3:18-20 NLT)

In Genesis, the second creation account suggests that the first man is lonely without a companion. What happens next is amazing! "Then the Lord God said, 'It is not good for the man to be alone. I will make a helper who is just right for him.' So the Lord God formed from the ground all the wild animals and all the birds of the sky. He brought them to the man to see what he would call them, and the man chose a name for each one. He gave names to all the livestock, all the birds of the sky, and all the wild animals. But still there was no helper just right for him" (Gen. 2:18-20 NLT). Cree theologian Ray Aldred suggests that the birds and animals are mentioned because an intimate relationship between humans and creation is already assumed.[8] The animals in the story are formed out of the same earth as humans, sharing the same mother earth and father God as human beings. The story then tells us that the man names the animals, again suggesting the intimacy of shared relationship and interdependence.

I would suggest that less relational views of reciprocity between humans and creation are modern misunderstandings, and they have everything to do with modern humanity's alienation from creation. As global development and urbanization continue, humans continue to lose their contact with the earth and her creatures. We find ourselves staring out of windows, looking at concrete, brick, and blacktop more often than we find ourselves standing in fields or forest and observing other parts of creation in the way Jesus did.

The artificial reality created by modernity places us in a world where human achievement is heralded as the pinnacle of beauty, wisdom, and inspiration. In our current worldview, human achievement, not God's creation, is seen as life's normative experience. One obvious example of Christianity's embrace of modernity, with incredible theological consequences, is the design of church buildings. Christian churches have adopted the practice of shutting creation out of their worship services rather than incorporating architectural designs that allow creation — God's first discourse of inspiration, wisdom, and beauty — to catch worshipers' attention and inspire them to recognize the Creator through the creation.

8. "Theology of the Land Conference," George Fox University, during a panel discussion consisting of the author, Ray Aldred, and Richard Twiss, February 7, 2011.

Church sanctuaries are enclosed, often without windows; or if they have windows, people color them with stained glass as if our human works of art could be greater than God's natural artistry.

As we move along the trajectory of modern history we seem to value the sacredness of creation less. Today, the natural world has become unfamiliar and even strange to us. Most of the thoughts we entertain concerning what we reference as "nature" are now twisted toward thoughts of chores, hunting excursions, and recreation in which we *challenge* nature and ultimately *conquer* nature (as if we could conquer God's creation!). Examples of failed disaster cleanups, such as in Valdez, Alaska, or the more recent Gulf oil spill, should teach us that nature cannot be easily conquered. But creation can be destroyed.

As modern humans continue our mass extraction of the earth's resources, including water, oil, coal, trees, metals, and minerals, we are failing to realize that we are reaching a tipping point. Humanity should have learned its lessons from the plight of the dodo and the passenger pigeon. When some things on earth are exploited too long, they can never recover. But in our modern world human greed does not take into account such boundaries.

As people of faith, we should view every drop of oil, every diamond, every lump of coal, and every source of water with a theological eye. We should try seeing our world through the eyes of the One who created it. All the earth is sacred. It seems quite foolish that only after we have gone too far will we realize that no amount of capital gains, no particular economic system, no modern convenience will be worth the price that we will be forced to pay. Attributed as a Cree Indian proverb, around Indian country they say, "Only when the last tree has died and the last river been poisoned and the last fish been caught will we realize we cannot eat money."[9] I sometimes wonder if modern humanity will drive itself to extinction over greed.

Modern, Euro-western, hierarchical worldviews set humanity up, over and above the rest of creation. In such a view it makes no sense to become intimate with creation. Taking time from our busy schedules in order to learn from animals, birds, fish, trees, earth, or a river seems very "unnatural" and artificial in our modern world. To the Euro-western mind nature is to be feared, conquered, killed, or utilized for its material value; it is never to be viewed as intimately related to us or sacred. While creation

9. http://www.facebook.com/pages/Native-American-Indian-Wisdom/298826369043?sk=info, accessed last on May 31, 2011.

may elicit inspirational feelings in people, to the Euro-western mind, animals, birds, water, and earth are rarely seen as the start of a continuous conversation with the Creator. The western view of creation has proven to be pitifully anthropocentric and utilitarian. Christianity has simply followed suit.

The Futility of Utility

At some level everyone enjoys the beauty found in creation. But even within an inspired view, I often hear people express a creation theology reflective of human-centered utility. In a utilitarian worldview nature is predominately thought of as being made for the purposes surrounding human function or for human pleasure. This type of assumption can even be expressed in heartfelt thoughts of God, in an attitude of thankfulness for God creating our world. No doubt such views are a part of God's purpose or we would not enjoy nature so much, but at the end of the day such views are more about differentiation between us and nature, over and above any kind of relational affiliation with creation. In some great reversal of rationale, modern humanity now thinks of creation primarily in terms of what it does for us, rather than seeing it as an inspiration for us to think of the greatness of God.

My friend Jim Sequeira told me about an experience he had when visiting an artist's store just off the beach in Southern California. Jim had spent a great deal of time admiring the artist's work, but then he had to admit to the artist that he could not afford to buy any of his beautiful art. "That's okay," replied the artist. "While it's true I make a living by selling my art, what I really enjoy is watching people admire it." Undoubtedly, the Creator makes "good stuff" so we can enjoy it. But aesthetic beauty is not the only reason for creation.

Regardless of whether one counts days or millennia in Genesis chapter 1, humans are still the final characters to show up in the story. Coming in last place should give us all pause for creaturely humility. We should realize that everything created was not made primarily for human happiness. Obviously, creation was enjoyed prior to our arrival. Consider the fact that there are places in the depth of the oceans, on the highest mountains, and deep in space that human beings have never seen and likely never will. Such unreachable places seem to be reserved for the Creator's enjoyment and for other beings in creation — but not for humans.

Creation exists for far more than our pleasure. In fact, if things continue down the road they are on, it will be easy to imagine a world operating in its fullness, but without the human beings that once inhabited it. Our anthropocentric worldviews can hardly bear the thought of the world not revolving around us. Though it should be said again, like all the other parts of creation, humans have an important place of connectedness to, for, and with creation. Part of our role is that of a protector and restorer of creation. I suggest we take our role more seriously if we are to continue living on this planet.

By following the Genesis chapter 1 creation story in its context, we can see that there is an obvious relationship between the Creator, the earth, human beings, animals, birds, plants, waters, and so on. As I pointed out earlier, the God who took time to create and observe natural goodness in its fullness also remains with creation. God doesn't abandon any of creation to be left on its own. After all, why would one create and hang a beautiful painting, never to take a second look?

In a similar fashion to the Genesis chapter 1 account, the writer of Psalm 148 (NLT) slowly unpacks and seems to enjoy what God has made.

Praise the LORD!

Praise the LORD from the heavens!
　　Praise him from the skies!
Praise him, all his angels!
　　Praise him, all the armies of heaven!
Praise him, sun and moon!
　　Praise him, all you twinkling stars!
Praise him, skies above!
　　Praise him, vapors high above the clouds!
Let every created thing give praise to the LORD,
　　for he issued his command, and they came into being.
He set them in place forever and ever.
　　His decree will never be revoked.

Praise the LORD from the earth,
　　you creatures of the ocean depths,
fire and hail, snow and clouds,
　　wind and weather that obey him,
mountains and all hills,

> fruit trees and all cedars,
> wild animals and all livestock,
>   small scurrying animals and birds,
> kings of the earth and all people,
>   rulers and judges of the earth,
> young men and young women,
>   old men and children.
>
> Let them all praise the name of the LORD.
>   For his name is very great;
>   his glory towers over the earth and heaven!
> He has made his people strong,
>   honoring his faithful ones —
>   the people of Israel who are close to him.
>
> Praise the LORD!

The psalmist reflects the Creator's enjoyment by recognizing the many aspects of how God is seen and glorified through creation. Each line reminds us to be thankful for such great gifts. It is truly humbling to know that God wants to share creation's beauty with us as we take the time to watch the beauty of creation unfold around us.

Native Americans have constructs similar to the scriptural examples of thanksgiving that honor the Creator for what he has done. One of those prayers, the *Haudenosaunee Thanksgiving Address,* has been formalized, and had I the space I would share all of it with you. In it, you would notice the great similarities in recognizing and enjoying each part of creation. The prayer representatively addresses every element of creation such as the people, the earth, the waters, the stars, the winds, and the birds; and at the end of each thought says "now our minds are one." Here is just one section of the long prayer:

> The Animals: We gather our minds together to send greetings and thanks to all the Animal life in the world. They have many things to teach us as people. We see them near our homes and in the deep forests. We are glad they are still here and we hope that it will always be so. Now our minds are one.[10]

10. 1993, provided here courtesy of Six Nations Indian Museum and the Tracking Proj-

Neither Native Americans, nor any indigenous peoples for that matter, have exclusive claims on understanding and relating to creation. Certainly there have been people in every generation, in all parts of the world, who attest to the Creator's witness through creation. Saint Francis of Assisi, who walked the earth in the early twelfth century, was one such European. Known as the patron saint of animals, Francis is reported to have preached to birds and negotiated an agreement with a ravenous wolf. Here is a portion of his *Canticle of the Sun*:

> Most high, all powerful, all good Lord! All praise is yours, all glory, all honor, and all blessing. To you, alone, Most High, do they belong. No mortal lips are worthy to pronounce your name.
>
> Be praised, my Lord, through all your creatures, especially through my lord Brother Sun, who brings the day; and you give light through him. And he is beautiful and radiant in all his splendor! Of you, Most High, he bears the likeness.
>
> Be praised, my Lord, through Sister Moon and the stars; in the heavens you have made them, precious and beautiful.
>
> Be praised, my Lord, through Brothers Wind and Air, and clouds and storms, and all the weather, through which you give your creatures sustenance.
>
> Be praised, My Lord, through Sister Water; she is very useful, and humble, and precious, and pure.
>
> Be praised, my Lord, through Brother Fire, through whom you brighten the night. He is beautiful and cheerful, and powerful and strong.
>
> Be praised, my Lord, through our sister Mother Earth, who feeds us and rules us, and produces various fruits with colored flowers and herbs.[11]

The psalmists, the writer of Genesis chapter 1, Saint Francis, and Native American prayers all seem to agree that the Creator has made a good

---

ect, *Thanksgiving Address: Greetings to the Natural World,* http://www.thetrackingproject .org/peacemaking/trackingtheroots.htm, last accessed on May 31, 2011. English version: John Stokes and Kanawahienton (David Benedict, Turtle Clan/Mohawk). Mohawk version: Rokwaho (Dan Thompson, Wolf Clan/Mohawk). Original inspiration: Tekaronianekon (Jake Swamp, Wolf Clan/Mohawk). Thanksgiving Address Fund, c/o Tracking Project, P.O. Box 266, Corrales, New Mexico 87048.

11. http://www.webster.edu/~barrettb/canticle.htm, last accessed on May 31, 2011.

world in which we are to live, be connected to, and thoroughly enjoy. God's first discourse is always present in creation, but the critical question in our generation is really more about how we are to live in God's world. The question is of infinite concern. How we view our role determines our answer. Is the world made for us or are we made as just one part of the creation? We must be careful how we answer because there may be a tendency for those who view creation primarily in a utilitarian way, to also view other people in a utilitarian way.

Ultimately, a utilitarian view of creation results in wanton destruction of the earth for the purposes of material gain. This attitude often crosses the realm of nature to people. A highly utilitarian view of people may explain why human life is valued so little in businesses that poison humanity (usually the poor and communities of color). Our view of creation may determine why international trade is accompanied by a propensity toward violence, wars, and even genocide. Invariably, the poorest and most marginalized on earth suffer the most from corporate imperialism's gathering of the earth's resources. Such actions often result in wholesale racism and injustice toward ethnic minorities. If diversity in creation is not understood and appreciated by those in the modern world, then perhaps it is not difficult to see why diversity would be of any value when considering others in humanity. There is a definite connection.

North American indigenous views and ancient Semitic worldviews, as represented in Scripture, find agreement in the understanding that creation is sacred. To the indigenous peoples of North America, our land and all it contains is *the* Holy Land. The land is sacred (holy) because it was given to us from the Creator, to be held in a trust relationship. The land is holy because God is holy. It is sacred because the land, and all creation, is considered to be a gift from God. Christians ought to be the first ones to realize this — after all, Christ is the Creator.

The Creator-Son and Reconciler

According to several writers in the Second Testament, Jesus is recognized as the Creator. The structure of those references to Christ as Creator are all possibly in a formulaic style, meaning they might have been memorized as poetic forms or sung as hymns. These formulaic patterns suggest that the early understanding of Christ as Creator was a popular theme in the early church. Here is the disciple John's account.

In the beginning the Word already existed. The Word was with God, and the Word was God. He existed in the beginning with God. God created everything through him, and nothing was created except through him. The Word gave life to everything that was created, and his life brought light to everyone. (John 1:1-4 NLT)

In John's mind, Jesus is preexistent; Jesus is God; Jesus was God's instrument in creation; and Jesus gave life to all creation. In the same chapter, verses 10-14 speak of God's redemptive value in Christ. John, who walked with Jesus, seems to have a fluid understanding of Jesus the man and Jesus the preexistent Christ as Creator. John also understands the very same Jesus as the Redeemer of all things. In a similar formulaic pattern to John's reference, Paul writes,

Christ is the visible image of the invisible God. He existed before anything was created and is supreme over all creation, for through him God created everything in the heavenly realms and on earth. He made the things we can see and the things we can't see — such as thrones, kingdoms, rulers, and authorities in the unseen world. Everything was created through him and for him. He existed before anything else, and he holds all creation together. Christ is also the head of the church, which is his body. He is the beginning, supreme over all who rise from the dead. So he is first in everything. For God in all his fullness was pleased to live in Christ, and through him God reconciled everything to himself. He made peace with everything in heaven and on earth by means of Christ's blood on the cross. (Col. 1:15-20 NLT)

In the Colossians passage Paul understands:

- Christ as the representative God
- Christ as preexistent
- Christ as having supremacy over all creation
- Christ as God's instrument in creation
- All creation as being created by Christ
- All creation made for Christ
- Christ making shalom with all creation by his redemptive atonement.

Paul's understanding parallels John's understanding of Christ the human, Christ the Creator, and Christ the Redeemer — or as Paul says elsewhere, Christ the reconciler of all things. Paul references another formulaic description of Christ as Creator in 1 Corinthians 8:6: "But we know that there is only one God, the Father, who created everything, and we live for him. And there is only one Lord, Jesus Christ, through whom God made everything and through whom we have been given life" (NLT). Once again, Paul states that through Jesus Christ, God made all creation, and through Christ we all have life.

A fourth reference, possibly constructed in the same or at least a similar kind of song, poem, or formula, is found in the book of Hebrews:

> Long ago God spoke many times and in many ways to our ancestors through the prophets. And now in these final days, he has spoken to us through his Son. God promised everything to the Son as an inheritance, and through the Son he created the universe. (Heb. 1:1-2 NLT)

The writer of Hebrews begins by reasoning that, through Christ, God created all of creation and that all creation belongs to him. Later, the same writer (Heb. 2:10) ties the creation act to Christ's redemptive actions by saying, "For it was fitting that he, for whom and by whom all things exist, in bringing many sons to glory, should make the founder of their salvation perfect through suffering" (ESV).

In this great mystery of incarnation and redemption, those who walked with or near the incarnated Christ came to a clear understanding that he was also the orchestrator of creation.[12] It may have even been common for many of the writers of the Second Testament to view Jesus as an incarnate human, as Christ the efficacious Creator, and as Christ the ultimate shalom, the one who restores all things and in whom all things are restored. Western theology has traditionally shown a weak understanding of Jesus as Creator. I would suggest that without a better understanding of God's plan through Jesus Christ as both Creator and as Savior/Restorer-Redeemer (shalom bringer), we in the modern church may have overzealously developed an imbalanced salvation theology.

The Creator of *all things* is also the redeemer or reconciler of *all things,* and *all things* (read all creation) are being created for Christ. Paul, in the Colossians passage, even says Christ "holds *all things together.*" It may be said that since *all things* are redeemable in Christ, then restoring the world

---

12. For a more complete historical theology, see Sean M. McDonough, *Christ as Creator: Origins of a New Testament Doctrine* (Oxford: Oxford University Press, 2009).

to shalom is the point of Christ's redemption. The basic issue is the breadth of healing God has made available in Christ. If Jesus died for all creation, and not just the human "soul," and not even just for humans, then the concept of redemption is much broader than many Christians have traditionally thought. Redemption (our salvation) is for the whole earth.

In the Cherokee language we have a phrase that points to Jesus as the *Creator-Son.*[13] This linguistic construction references Jesus' sonship, in relation to the Father, while at the same time referencing his role in creation. In this simple formula Jesus is acknowledged as both divine Creator and divine Son. The implications of embracing this broader understanding, of Christ as the one who creates all things and as the one who restores all things, has tremendous missional significance.

Monotheistic peoples have prayed to the Creator of all things for millennia without ever knowing the Second Testament claim that Jesus Christ is the historic Creator. Put simply, if indigenous peoples have been praying to the Creator and the Creator is Christ, to whom have they been praying? Asked in another way, since there exist among indigenous peoples numerous testimonies of the Creator's intervention and blessing in their lives, with whom have they been in relationship?

Certainly a broader missional view would have been good news to such people. Instead, indigenous peoples were most often told by Euro-western missionaries that they worshiped another god. One also wonders what has been the effect of a theology that separates the Creator-Son and Savior/Restorer of all things? Such an imbalance has prevented western theologians from understanding a broader view of salvation and has helped maintain a dualism that prevents people from understanding that all creation, together, comes under the covering of Christ's universal restoration.

Based on the past missional perspectives, the result of such an imbalanced theology is apparent — a weak salvation theology equals a weak god. A weak god is not great enough to reach all peoples everywhere or able to restore all creation. The god of western mission has too often been capricious, carrying with him an exceptionalist theology that favors the categories and conclusions of the Euro-western world. Perhaps God is greater than the west has presumed. There is nowhere that we can travel, including the depths of the ocean or outer space, where Christ is not active in creation. It would seem that part of our job on earth is to discover what Christ is up to, and to join him in it!

13. *Oo-nay-thla-nah-hee Yo-way-jee.*

Mapping Out Creation's Future

Today is a new day of theological possibilities. New possibilities are arising as our former, weaker theological categories are being reexamined by nonwestern eyes and minds. Nonwestern peoples are discovering that the theologies bent toward a western doctrinal trajectory may limit the bigness of God and who God is in Jesus Christ. Indigenous peoples have been told for centuries that our historic relationship to the Creator was suspect at best, and demonic at worst. It is time to remove the log from the western hegemonic theological enterprise, prior to removing the splinter from nonwestern and indigenous theological constructs. Brave new theological partnerships and open minds are needed for the twenty-first century. If we wish to live out shalom together (Euro-west and non-west), we must realize we are all on a journey together with Christ to heal the world. The caveat is, we must all be willing to put down our "pet" theologies, because they are embedded in the traditions of the west.

Pope John Paul II came to a startling realization: "Over the years I have become more and more convinced that the ideologies of evil are profoundly rooted in the history of European philosophical thought."[14] The anthropocentric dualism between material and spiritual reality, as widely understood in the Euro-western world, has fed into the idea of a disposable earth and disposable societies. That is, Euro-western dualism has produced an attitude that "as long as it is not my society, my community, or my family experiencing the ramifications, I can ignore it." Even western ecological worldviews, as helpful as they can be under certain circumstances, may not offer anything better in the end than social narcissism.

There are a number of hurdles that the western world and worldviews will need to clear in order to preserve creation and find shalom in the community of creation. These hurdles include:

- the Platonic and Cartesian dualisms that lead us to value reason over experience, and the spiritual over the "secular" or the material, etc.
- the oppressive pedagogies that promote dualistic tenets
- extrinsic categorization over relational categorization that leads to creating false realities removed from the whole

14. Fr. James V. Schall, S.J., "Benedict on Aquinas: 'Faith Implies Reason,'" February 1, 2007, http://www.ignatiusinsight.com/features2007/print2007/schall_b16aquinas_feb07 .html, last accessed on May 31, 2011.

- a "progressive" view of civilization that understands ancient peoples to be less civilized than modern peoples
- an anthropocentric worldview where humans dominate nature
- neocolonialism, which includes economic coercion and military violence as a substitute for true, democratic, relationally based authority
- individual greed, expressed through unbridled and unchecked capitalism, which has led to the commodification of people and natural resources, including land, water, and even air, over the interest of the common good of all
- twofold judgments, which have been defined as follows:

> A special characteristic of western thinking, fully reflected in American ways, is that of making twofold judgments based on principle. The structure of the Indo-European languages seems to foster this kind of thinking and the action that follows. A situation is assigned to a category held high, thus providing a justification for positive effort, or to one held low, with justification for rejection, avoidance, or other negative action. Twofold judgments seem to be the rule in western and American life: moral-immoral, legal-illegal, right-wrong, sin-virtue, success-failure, clean-dirty, civilized-primitive, practical-impractical, introvert-extrovert, and secular-religious, Christian-pagan. This kind of thinking tends to put the world of values into absolutes, and its arbitrary nature is indicated by the fact that modern science no longer uses opposite categories, in almost all instances preferring to use the concept of a range with degrees of difference separating the poles.[15]

Many of the existing forms of the environmental movement will be helpful in the short run, but unless they become rooted in a familial love of creation, I fear that they are simply representing a sanitized version of utilitarianism. As Tracy Chapman's song reminds us, we are related to the earth, and the earth is our mother: "Mother of us all / Place of our birth / How can we stand aside / And watch the rape of the world."[16]

Whether the term "Mother Earth" is helpful in a literal way or as a

15. Conrad M. Arensberg and Arthur H. Niehoff, "American Cultural Values," in Conrad M. Arensberg and Arthur H. Niehoff, eds., *Introducing Social Change* (Chicago: Aldine Publishing Co., 1971), 210-14.

16. From "Rape of the World" by Tracy Chapman, from the album, "New Beginning," copyright 1995.

metaphor, the logical relationship is present; we all come from the earth and to the earth we will all return. When all human beings lose this sense of commonality, we lose our balance and our humanity. When the colonizers forget their relationship to the earth (perhaps through philosophical parsing or simply callousness), it gives them a powerful weapon over those they intend to colonize. Native author Andrea Smith, in her book *Conquest: Sexual Violence and American Indian Genocide,* makes the case for the unjust use of power during colonization of Native American lands, paralleling the power used to assert rights over Native American bodies. John Mohawk, *Thinking in Indian: A John Mohawk Reader* (edited by Jose Barreiro), colors the language with the idea of torturing the land and torturing the people. When one group of humans neglects to think about the earth as our mother, even while knowing that another group views it as such, they can for a while rape, kill, and torture the very root of a people's existence. Unfortunately, regardless of their state of mind, they are doing the same thing to themselves as well.

The apostle Paul uses the concept of the earth as our mother in Romans 8:22. "For we know that all creation has been groaning as in the pains of childbirth right up to the present time" (NLT). Without breaking through the dualistic Euro-western categories, many environmentalists will continue to view creation as something apart from themselves. Such views are more about sustaining nature for prolonged use and not as much about a familial relationship with creation. With that said, there are some similarities to indigenous ideas and ideologies of earthkeeping found in environmental movements like Deep Ecology/Ecosophy. For example, I find some agreement among indigenous views and ecosophical views, including understandings that:

- All life is interconnected and reciprocal.
- Human beings have a symbiotic relationship with creation.
- Life is biocentric *in that* each part has a role to play in the natural relationship of harmony.
- Creation teaches values for living and learning.
- We can appreciate the quality of life we enjoy without needing to move toward higher standards (a.k.a. "progress").

Indigenous views may differ from Deep Ecology in the following understandings:

- Creation exists because of a Creator or Sacred Force (the Great Mystery).
- Life is intrinsically valuable *because* it is a gift from the Creator and therefore it is sacred, meaning that purpose is crucial to existence.
- Life is not *just* biocentric; it also has a slightly anthropocentric side. The role of human beings is unique, and humans relate to the rest of creation uniquely. This view might be described as *ministrocentric*[17] (centered on serving creation, maintaining harmony, assuring reciprocity, and conducting ceremonies of mediation, etc., in order to maintain harmony and restore harmony whenever it is broken). This includes restoring harmony through gratitude, reciprocity, and ceremony between the Creator, humans, and all other parts of creation.
- Creation does not exist to be in isolation, but creation is the Creator's first discourse — in which humanity has a seat of learning and in which the discourse is continuous.
- Harmony is not simply understood as a philosophy among most indigenes; it is more about how life operates, and it is the only way that life can continue, if life is to be lived as the Creator intends.

Postmodern and Indigenous

We are now at a point in human history when we must realize that modernity, in all its forms, especially as expressed in the Euro-western world, was "Dead On Arrival." The industrial age and neocolonialism, following the era of colonialism, have written a check to our world that has insufficient funds. We are doomed if we don't change our course. Only a worldview encompassing the interconnectedness between Creator, human beings, and the rest of creation as one family is adequate. Such a worldview is fundamentally indigenous and biblical. Our survival as a people on this planet may depend on its adoption. If we are wise, we will follow the lead of indigenous peoples who are bringing forth empowering movements, such as Bolivia's proposed "Law of Mother Earth." At the time of this writing, Bolivia is set to be the first nation to enact a law giving the earth similar rights as humans.

> The country, which has been pilloried by the U.S. and Britain in the U.N. climate talks for demanding steep carbon emission cuts, will es-

17. *Ministro,* meaning to serve, wait upon, provide, supply.

tablish 11 new rights for nature. They include: the right to life and to exist; the right to continue vital cycles and processes free from human alteration; the right to pure water and clean air; the right to balance; the right not to be polluted; and the right to not have cellular structure modified or genetically altered. Controversially, it will also enshrine the right of nature "to not be affected by mega-infrastructure and development projects that affect the balance of ecosystems and the local inhabitant communities." "It makes world history. Earth is the mother of all," said Vice-President Alvaro García Linera. "It establishes a new relationship between man and nature, the harmony of which must be preserved as a guarantee of its regeneration."[18]

The "Law of Mother Earth," as it is being called, grew out of the World People's Conference on Climate Change held in Cochabamba, Bolivia, in April 2010. The gathering was a response to the failure of the climate talks in Copenhagen to allow the world's indigenous voices to be heard during the 15th United Nations Conference in December 2009. Proposals for U.N. adoption of laws protecting the earth were presented a year after the Cochabamba gathering. Bolivia is one of many struggling countries trying to deal with its weather anomalies such as rising temperatures, melting glaciers, numerous floods, droughts, and mudslides. Bolivia, like many other nations (including the U.S.) is a battleground country between the rights of indigenous peoples, especially landless peoples, and a corrupt and violent Corporate State. It is no accident that a law to protect Mother Earth arose after the election of Evo Morales, Latin America's first indigenous president.

I understand the single conceptual integration of land, history, religion, and culture may be difficult for many western minds to embrace. For Native Americans, this integration is often explained as a visceral "knowing" or as somehow embedded in our DNA. This feeling we have of ourselves as a people, including our history and cultures being connected to the land, is perhaps the single most glaring difference between a Eurowestern worldview and an indigenous Native North American worldview. But if we are all to survive the twenty-first century, things must change,

18. This article was published on guardian.co.uk at 18.17 BST on Sunday, April 10, 2011. A version appeared on p. 15 of the main section of the *Guardian* on Monday, April 11, 2011. http://www.guardian.co.uk/environment/2011/apr/10/bolivia-enshrines-natural-worlds -rights?INTCMP=SRCH, last accessed on May 31, 2011.

even among our Euro-western friends, so that they can sense a similar connection. How does such a paradigm shift happen?

All people must begin to view the earth as our mother, God as our Father, and all the creatures on the earth as our relatives. After all, we have the same Creator. Both shalom and the Native American Harmony Way make room for the kind of living that creates an atmosphere of respect in which these relationships can exist. God, through Christ, created the entire earth and everything in it. Everything in creation plays a part in the others' existence and well-being.

One of the most basic examples of this kind of reciprocity is how the exchange of oxygen and carbon dioxide between plants and animals keeps us all living. So, in a simple paradigm, such as the symbiotic reciprocity between plants and the creation of oxygen, we naturally understand that all things created need each other in order to live in harmony. We are all related. What would our responsible role be in this simple example? Curb the cutting of the world's forests and develop sustainable alternatives.

Reciprocity is a natural law of the universe. For humans to maintain harmony, we must reflect the reciprocity in the created order. There is fluidity between understanding reciprocity between human beings and reciprocity of all other parts of creation. For example, concerning people: when we choose to help others in our community, it often comes back around to us. Likely, someone will end up helping us when we need it; but even if they don't, the reward is built into the initial act by how we feel when we help someone else. Mutuality and natural reciprocity are appreciated by understanding that all of creation operates according to this principle. Another way to say this is that in all of life there is a harmonious existence and an existence of chaos. Harmony is the action that restores the balance and subsumes the chaos.

"Action" should become an important word in Euro-western people's vocabulary in order to remind us of the intimate connection with creation, and to break dualistic thinking. Euro-western people might also consider developing new ways of expressing their thanks through ceremony. Through expressing gratitude in ceremonies, indigenous peoples reveal to others and themselves the connection between the Creator, human beings, the earth, and all the rest of creation. A foundation of Native American ceremony is gratitude for the relationships that exist. Euro-western people need to rediscover what their indigenous ancestors once knew and, in so many ways, become indigenous once again. To move ahead, and perhaps simply to survive, we must all be connected to creation in harmony.

CHAPTER FOUR

We Are All Related: Life Governed by Harmony

1491 B.C. (Before Columbus)

Typical worldviews among traditional Native Americans are about maintaining harmony or balance in life.[1] This concern over a harmonious existence makes a way for one's happiness, health, and well-being. Harmony, present in both a worldview and a sense or feeling, is the hallmark of all Native American spirituality. How does such a concept survive the coldness of modernity? The effort to preserve our Native American ways is more difficult now than ever. Today, I sense a widespread feeling among traditional Native Americans that harmony is much more difficult to attain now than it was in the past. The reasons for the difficulty may seem complex to Christians who tend to blame most of humanity's problems on *the fall* of Adam and Eve in the garden of Eden.

Many traditional Indians view the story of the fall in the Genesis account as a story about Europeans. For Euro-westerners, the story of the fall explains something they fundamentally believe concerning humanity

---

1. I freely acknowledge that there is no one indigenous voice. We are many and varied, but we all have in common our context, and our primary worldview is nonwestern. As stated earlier, my conclusions about indigenous life-ways of harmony and balance are drawn from my own experiences, those experiences of conversing on the subject with other indigenous peoples, and from the literature review, research conclusions, etc., of my Ph.D. dissertation. I also acknowledge that many nonindigenous, western thinkers have addressed similar concerns of harmony and balance in life and have made valuable contributions to this conversation.

called "human depravity." A popular Native American belief is that we, who were here in America, never left our garden of Eden. With this background in mind, it doesn't take much imagination to figure out who replaces the snake as the interloper in the Eden story. Clearly, the Europeans who landed here without regard for the civilizations in place are the ones sent to do evil.

I am not convinced that the Eden myth explains what Euro-western theologians call "human depravity" as much as it explains what many indigenous people understand as disequilibrium. Myth is not about whether something is fact or fiction; myth is more about truth. Good myth, according to the old adage, is about something that continues to be true again and again, over time. What is true about Eden?

Author Brian McLaren talks about a six-line narrative that has been misappropriated from classic Greek philosophy and co-opted onto the Hebrew myth in Genesis.[2] McLaren groups the following stages together in both traditions:

1. Eden/Platonic Ideal
2. Fall/Cave of Illusion
3. Condemnation/Aristotelian Real-Becoming
4. Hell-Damnation/Greek Hades
5. Salvation/Salvation
6. Heaven/Platonic Ideal[3]

According to McLaren, reading history backwards, through the six-line narrative, distracts us from some basic truths that God has been trying to teach us about the Jewish story. I believe something similar has been done as the West "read back" into Native American theology. Perhaps shalom, and the disequilibrium that results in broken shalom, is closer to what the author of Genesis is trying to teach us. I think Native Americans, and possibly many other peoples, can find more agreement with the shalom or harmony narrative than with any type of conclusion containing inherited sin and human depravity.

Do Native Americans view life as perfect or utopian prior to the European invasion? Not at all. It is not that we don't recognize the concept of

---

2. Brian D. McLaren, *A New Kind of Christianity: Ten Questions That Are Transforming the Faith* (New York: HarperOne, 2010).

3. McLaren, *A New Kind of Christianity*, 34, 41.

sinfulness, even though many Native American traditions say they have no word for sin in their language. But sin looks different to Native Americans than it appears in traditional European doctrinal concepts. Sin needn't be inherited or permanent for it to be present in everyone. Characteristically, similar ideas of mistake-making may be found among Native Americans. Generally, we view sin a bit differently. Among traditional Native Americans, restoring broken harmony is less individualistic, being more about restoring the community — less guilt ridden, not inherent, more tangibly rectifiable, and much more oriented toward restoring harmonious relationships in all of creation, rather than simply obtaining human forgiveness.

A Cherokee elder once told me, as he was commenting on how often our young people use smoke to cleanse themselves these days[4] (and I think he was counting me as a "young person"), that in the old days they used a cedar fire only two or three times a year to cleanse themselves. Then he paused, thought about it, and said, "Come to think of it, I think you guys need it a lot more now than we used to." The elder's understanding was consistent with the manifold references I have heard other elders make concerning the past. In their minds they view human mistakes as a good thing. All people make mistakes; this is the basis of being human. But we should always learn from our mistakes.

Many Native American prayers begin with similar words to these: "Creator, have pity (mercy) on me, remember that I am just a human being." To our people, being human is a good thing. When we forget our humanity and try to take the place of the Creator is when our actions are really shameful. Then, we must learn from our mistakes, often asking for help from the Creator and others around us. An Ojibwa elder I knew once told me, "The Christian ways and Ojibwa ways are much the same. But we [Ojibwa] don't have a concept of sin or hell. We make mistakes and we learn from them and we all go to the heaven place, the Happy Hunting Ground. When a person doesn't learn from their mistakes in this lifetime, sometimes it takes a little longer for them to get there. They have to wander for a while."

Making mistakes reminds us that we are made to be human and we are not God. In traditional Native American art forms, often a mistake is left in a rug, basket, or pottery as a way of reinforcing our humanity. The

---

4. Smoke from cedar and other plants is used by many Native American tribes as a symbol of prayer and cleansing.

logic of the mistakes is that if the mistakes were not visible, we might consider our work or ourselves to be perfect, like Creator. Native American belief is not about perfection but rather about our role or place in the universe.

I feel very blessed to have lived long enough to know Native American elders who spanned the premodern and modern ages. I remember as a young adult speaking to elders who were born in teepees and even one woman who was born in captivity among Geronimo's band after the Indian Wars. I have sat with elders who were given their names by an Indian agent, and with those who knew how to live with none of our modern conveniences. These elders grew up in an age without amenities such as electricity, indoor plumbing, automobiles, or schools. In their day, a trip to the "convenience store" was a once-per-month wagon ride across the Oklahoma hills to receive their rations from the Indian agent. The remainder of their groceries consisted of what they hunted and gathered.

The character of the people I am referring to was as strong as oak, but at the same time the people were as flexible as willow. Their beliefs were rooted in an understanding that life was more harmonious in the recent past, or at the least, that harmony was much easier to maintain prior to the European invasion. Amazingly, these esteemed elders adapted as necessary to modern life — some of them even after horrendous experiences of loss in their lives.

Today these type of elders are precious and few. Most of us, especially those of us in the "Indian Diaspora," who attempt to maintain some form of a traditional lifestyle, are caught in a "neotraditional" existence. We have become so dependent on the conveniences of modernity that we are willing to be complicit with colonialism here, and in other parts of the world, in order to maintain our own American level of comfort. All these cultural changes make it difficult to speak these days from a traditional perspective or even come close to the level of integrity imbued in our elders in generations past.

We who have heard their stories and who have known the people who experienced a truly indigenous way of life owe a debt to them to try our best to pass on to our children, and share with others, the wisdom they carried with them daily. I have never known someone who was truly traditional who did not want the best possible life, not just for themselves or their own tribal group, but for all peoples in the world. Living life from a Harmony Way is almost always the framework of such a good life.

What Is in a Word?

From my own experience among the Cherokee (my own tribal people), the concept of well-being is represented often in the word *Eloheh* (ay-luh-hay). *Eloheh* is one of several Cherokee words describing the concept of the Harmony Way or a shalom-type construct. In my doctoral dissertation process I was able to discover more about *Eloheh* and its connection to similar constructs used by other Native North Americans. In that study I explored the possibility that a restoration of the Harmony Way might be a source of healing for indigenous peoples, and might even provide hope for Euro-Americans who are leading very fractured lives.

Eloheh is translated as "Balance" or sometimes as the "Harmony Way." The actual translation is likely from a very sacred word *eloh'*, with the added *eh* at the end of the word making it a place. *Eloh'* is used to refer to Cherokee religion and even a much broader concept that includes our land, history, law, and culture.[5] In Cherokee, the Harmony Way is also said to be a way of *Duyukta,* which means something close to justice or righteousness. Sometimes in Cherokee the Harmony Way is simply referred to as "the Way." Based on my experience among the Eastern Cherokee, the *Duyukta* tends to be used as a verb and *Eloheh* used more as a noun. In other words, wherever Duyukta is lived out might be considered a place of Eloheh. Among the Oklahoma Cherokee, *Eloheh* is more likely to be used as both a way of life and a place. These terms are sometimes used separately in colloquial conversation, even though the full meaning of both may be inherent by using just one of the words. In the following example, an Eastern Cherokee elder describes *Duyukta* but could just as easily be describing *Eloheh.*

> The Cherokee believe that stories, along with ceremonies, arts and crafts, and other traditions, help the individual and the culture to "stay in balance." The Cherokee attribute their survival as a people, a unique culture, to their closeness to the land and their adherence to Duyukta. Duyukta is a moral code that might be roughly translated as "the right way," "the right path," or "the path of being in balance. . . ." It is the traditional Cherokee way of living: placing importance on the good of the whole more than the individual; having freedom but taking responsi-

---

5. Jace Weaver, *That the People Might Live: Native American Literatures and Native American Community* (Oxford: Oxford University Press, 1997), Preface.

bility for yourself; staying close to the earth and all our relations. And how does one do this? By taking time to dream; by understanding our nature and our needs and taking care of them; by doing ceremonies that keep us in balance like going to water and using the sweat lodge; by listening and praying; by recognizing our dark and light sides; by having the support of the family, extended family, clan, and tribe. The medicine people say it requires understanding ourselves and our place in the world around us.[6]

Another Cherokee, artist Jimmy Durham, in testimony to the U.S. Congress, described the symbiotic nature of all that Cherokees do and who we are by using the term *Eloheh.*

> I am a Cherokee. In the language of my people there is a word for land: Eloheh. This same word also means history, culture, and religion. We cannot separate our place on the Earth from our lives on the Earth, nor from our vision and our meaning as a people. We are taught from childhood that the animals and plants [which] we share a place with are our brothers and sisters. . . . Today the Tennessee Valley Authority plans to flood the sacred valley that held our two principal cities. . . . The anthropologists have dug up some bones and some pottery at Achota and TVA tells us that we can visit these bones at a museum. But the spirits of our ancestors are not in a museum. They live in the pine and hickory and walnut trees, and in those free-running creeks and rivers. . . . This incredible arrogance toward other life has caused great destruction in this country. . . . The Cherokee people are of one voice and of one mind that this dam, this degradation, be stopped. We want our universe, our Eloheh, with all its fish and all its life, to continue. And we are sure that this cannot be against the interests and wishes of the American people![7]

6. Barbara R. Duncan, ed., *Living Stories of the Cherokee* (Chapel Hill: University of North Carolina Press, 1998), 25.

7. Jimmy Durham, Cherokee activist's testimony on the TVA Tellico Dam Congressional hearings, as quoted in "Some Crucial Issues of Our Time" by Nicholas G. L. Guppy, M.A. (Cantab.), M.A. (Oxon.), The Pond, Haddenham, Cambridgeshire CB6 3XD, United Kingdom, 6-7. http://journals.cambridge.org/action/displayAbstract;jsessionid=0A86EA16 C1EC1EAE23BC7F86E859DC64.tomcat1?fromPage=online&aid=5923600, last accessed on May 31, 2011.

Among Native Americans it is a generally held belief that our elders and spiritual leaders are considered closest to being what the western world would call experts. Our elders and spiritual leaders are the most reliable sources of knowledge and considered the authoritative repository of spiritual traditions. In my dissertation process I interviewed eight Native North American spiritual leaders/elders from various tribal backgrounds.[8] In each interview I began with the same statement, saying: "In my own Cherokee culture we have a concept of harmony and balance we call 'Eloheh.' It's how life is supposed to be lived in the way Creator intended." After my initial statement, I kept silent. The first point was to see whether or not they recognized such a concept in their own tribal culture and then, to allow them to talk about it without interruption. In every case the interviewees seemed to know exactly what I was talking about and then proceeded to expound on their own understanding of harmony in their particular tribal context.

Learning from my own intertribal experiences, I had some small understanding that other tribes also used a harmony concept as a foundation for living. I found that each tribe has a word or several words in its own language that broadly represent living in harmony and balance. As far as English references go, some tribes speak of harmony as a way of balance; some refer to the concept as the "beauty way"; while others may talk of a "good way" or "good road" or "good path." Other tribal groups call it the "blessing way." The majority of Native American people tend to recognize the concept in their own tribes and in other tribes. Another pan-Indian reference to such a harmony way is the "Red Road." In Cherokee it is also sometimes called the "White Path."

It may not be an overstatement to assume that other indigenous peoples around the world, but not all, have understandings of the Harmony Way very similar to North American indigenous peoples. Anthropologist Darrell Whiteman makes a similar observation of the kind of shalom-like life construct among indigenous people in a Melanesian context.

8. The U.S. Federal Government recognizes over 560 tribal entities in the United States, not counting the many tribal groups who are not federally recognized. A similar scenario would be true for Canada. Each of these tribal nations may or may not have a well-being concept, but because of the vast possibilities that existed, I wanted to interview elders/spiritual leaders representing a wide geographic profile. The interviewees were all Native North American elders/spiritual leaders or at least burgeoning elders/spiritual leaders who know their own culture well, and in most cases, who know of other tribal cultures and ideas. The only question I asked was one that allowed them to identify a concept of harmony in their own culture or other cultures.

The Hebrew concept of Shalom — physical and spiritual wellbeing, reconciliation, justice — comes close to capturing the essence of this central Melanesian value. Human beings are the central focus of cosmic life — the centre of the Melanesian universe — but it is inclusive of plants, animals, inorganic matter and spirit beings, all belonging to an integrated universe pulsating with energy. Ancestors are perceived as the living dead, playing an active role in this cosmic life. The categories of life and death, sacred and secular, animate and inanimate, do not have the same definite features for a Melanesian as Western man would give them.[9]

Whether we are referring to the Hebrew construct of shalom, the Native American Harmony Way, or other indigenous constructs like the Melanesian one described above, what may readily be observed among indigenous peoples is their holistic and integrative worldview. Western worldviews tend to be less integrative and more reflective of modernity's extrinsic categorization, as well as having an emphasis on the individual at the expense of the community.

Living Happily Ever . . . Now

People from the dominant western Euro-American culture don't like to hear Native Americans talk about how life was far happier before they arrived. I have been interrupted on numerous occasions by white students in my courses, and by white Christians in churches, who want to argue this point. Usually the argument begins in the form of a question such as, "Are you saying that Native Americans didn't have any sin before the white man came?" or they say something like, "You guys were all killing each other before we got here." Such arguments can easily be tempered with an understanding that the amount of goodness or badness in societies doesn't need to be viewed through a perspective of zero-sum gain. When discussing cultures, I think gradients of a society's goodness or badness are preferred concepts rather than an either/or approach.

Typically, Euro-Americans cast aside the view of the elders that I ref-

9. Darrell Whiteman, *Melanesians and Missionaries: An Ethnohistorical Study of Social and Religious Change in the Southwest Pacific* (Pasadena, Calif.: William Carey Library, 1983), 65.

erence as an unrealistic and romantic view of the Native American past. Euro-Americans have a difficult time believing that Native Americans prefer much of their own past to the Eurocentric-dominated present. I don't believe a preferred, pre-European invasion view reflects a type of Native American utopianism as much as it acknowledges that there can be no way forward unless we reclaim the ways that worked so well for us in the past. This connection to the past is strong and pervasive among Native Americans, as pointed out by Professor Vine Deloria Jr.:

> Even the most severely eroded Indian community today still has a substantial fragment of the old ways left, and these ways are to be found in the Indian family. Even the badly shattered families preserve enough elements of kinship so that whatever the experiences of the young, there is a sense that life has some unifying principles that can be discerned through experience that guides behavior. This feeling, and it is a strong emotional feeling toward the world that transcends beliefs and information, continues to gnaw at American Indians throughout their lives.[10]

Deloria is speaking broadly of the "unifying principles" or what I refer to as Harmony Way values. But he also is addressing a specific feeling that connects Indians to the past. This is a difficult feeling to describe, but I believe he accurately points out the fact that it continues to "gnaw" at us, and it perhaps even makes us sick (read PTSD). The point I wish to establish is that in many ways, life in America was much better for Native Americans prior to 1492. While this has a lot to do with the values of the past, I want to make a case that it also has everything to do with the here and now.

For nonwestern peoples, the timeline between past and present is much more integrated than it is set in boundaries. Perhaps similar understandings can be illustrated in the Scriptures among the Hebrew prophets. Prophets such as Jeremiah were constantly calling the people back to remember past covenants, their stories and past sacred experiences. "Thus says the LORD, 'Stand by the ways and see and ask for the ancient paths, where the good way is, and walk in it; and you will find rest for your souls . . .'" (Jer. 6:16a).

---

10. Vine Deloria Jr. and Daniel R. Wildcat, *Power and Place: Indian Education in America* (Golden, Colo.: Fulcrum, 2001), 43.

While I am not saying that we should all "live *in* the past," that is to say, to live as if we are in another time, I am saying that we should not live as if the past has no bearing or reference to the here and now. Jeremiah's hopes were that his people would return to the sacred reference points from their past in order to live better into the present. This feeling of dissonance that premodern people, such as Native Americans, experience seemingly more often than westerners, may be similar to a sense I have heard modern Christians express in the idea of being a "pilgrim" or in the saying, "This world is not my home." Perhaps there is a similar cognitive dissonance felt by Native Americans because we must live in a world that we know was made for us by the Creator, but its systems and values have become subjugated to the values of the interloper — the dominant, modern, western society whose values are very different than ours.

According to the practicality of shalom, and according to our Native American Harmony Way, we were not made to experience divided loyalties between heaven and earth. God's intention has always been for us to make this earth fully our home. There exists in America a ubiquitous and foundationally dualistic theology behind the idea of living between heaven and earth. As human beings, I think that both the Native American and the ancient Semitic view on the subject is that we are made to experience the fullness of our relationship *with* the earth and *on* the earth. Perhaps a greater portion of Euro-western theology than we realize has become "so heavenly minded that it is no earthly good."

As I attempt to point out in the following poem, pitiable is the person who is caught in any dualism — torn between two lovers, always thinking about the one far off while remaining present with the one so near.

Indian in Another Place
by Randy Woodley

i find myself locked inside this concrete maze
to fulfill some ill-conceived expectation
chained to the conversations of ten thousand people saying nothing
together in bizarre concert my heart screams in silence
escape . . . find the earth and let her hold you before peace is elusive
and honor cannot be claimed.

*   *   *   *

the hostile city lights reflect against storefront mirrors
preaching the obscene echoes of obtrusive billboards

my eyes squint as they wound my soul and
i stand dizzy and bleeding
running faster and faster from the hostile pace set as a trap for me
still longing for the sacred places i know.

****

Great Spirit, make my feet run swiftly
open my eyes to the peace in clear blue skies,
my ears to the bird songs of joy and laughing water
allow me once again to breathe in the pleasures
of sweetgrass and fresh wet earth
and put me in a place where one word spoken from the heart
is heard for a lifetime.

For Native Americans (and, I will argue, for everyone else as well), the answer to the challenge of dualism is not to become assimilated into the modern world but to begin to experience life closer to how our premodern ancestors experienced it, literally "getting back to nature." When God said the earth is "really good," I think God meant it! The whole of creation is meant to be fully embraced each day, savoring each mountain sunset; holding onto the smell of fallen pine needles after a sudden storm; drinking in the sound of the ocean waves; and celebrating the reality that we are enjoying this creation right now, with all the rest of God's creatures on earth, and with the Creator.

Part of what made life in America better prior to 1492 was simply having an unmolested worldview in which people could live an integrated spirituality that connected each moment between the past and the present. The eternal aspects of creation remind us of this connection. In the past, there was no need to make categorical differentiations between time and space, because it was all lived together. Heaven and earth, and for that matter hell, were all to be experienced both now and later, but why worry about *later* when *now* is so abundantly full of life?

Redbird Smith, the man credited most for bringing back our Cherokee religion and traditions at a time when they were fading, said this about the future:

This religion does not teach me to concern myself of the life that shall be after this, but it does teach me to be concerned with what my everyday life should be. The Fires kept burning are merely the greater Fire, the greater Light, the Great Spirit. I realize now as never before it is not only for the Cherokees but for all mankind. (Redbird Smith, Chief of the Nighthawk Keetoowah, 1917)[11]

I can garner at least two principles reading Smith's words:

1. We should not worry about the future but we should live life today in all its fullness.
2. Religion is not solely an individual or even a "tribal" concern. What is true and good in one religion may be good for others as well.

The subject of the second point is dealt with elsewhere in this book. The first point sounds strikingly similar to the words of Jesus after pointing out how God takes care of the birds and the flowers in the field: "So don't worry about tomorrow, for tomorrow will bring its own worries. Today's trouble is enough for today" (Matt. 6:34 NLT). When coupled with Jesus' words in John 10:10b, "I came that they may have life, and have it abundantly," one can easily recognize the affinity between Jesus' concept of shalom and the Native American Harmony Way. Both constructs place God in the center as the provider.

The connection between heaven and earth is the way in which the Creator provides in abundance. The earth produces everything we need if human beings are willing to share its resources. When people hoard the earth's resources or despoil the earth, God's rich blessings become cursed. As a result, people no longer feel secure and feel they must set about protecting their seemingly scarce resources. Wars are waged over such concerns. In the end, the whole project reflects a lack of trust in the Creator. Left alone without the Creator's renewal and infusion of new lives, these systems of selfishness, mistrust, hoarding, polluting, and cursed thinking take on a life of their own and eventually they begin to breed subsidiary forms of oppression.

Systemic Oppression

The apostle Paul's idea of systemic demonic oppression in Ephesians chapter 6 indicates that these systems can be corrected by applying shalom/Harmony Way principles to our thinking. In Ephesians 6:13-15, using the

11. http://www.cherokee.org/Culture/70/Page/default.aspx, last accessed on May 31, 2011.

analogy of armor, Paul says, "[s]tand firm then, with the belt of truth buckled around your waist, with the breastplate of righteousness in place, and with your feet fitted with the readiness that comes from the gospel of peace." Though each "piece of armor" deserves interpretive rendering, I wish only to point out the connection between "righteousness" and the "good news of shalom."

Paul, a Jew, trained well in the sacred texts, understood a connection between the shalom way of living and the Hebrew Testament background concerning righteousness. In our modern dualistic theologies, righteousness is often understood as personal purity. Although the idea of personal holiness should not be excluded as part and parcel of the broader concept, Paul knew well that righteousness had the broader context of acting rightly toward one's community. He understood the background of the twin concepts of "justice" and "righteousness" and how they were actions for the common good of the community, creating systems of shalom. Conversely, Paul could see how evil overtakes the systems of a community and how it allows the systems to develop in demonic oppression rather than life-giving, shared systems of shalom.

Any system, starting out fairly good (whether from small systems like a family to large complex systems, like a whole culture), can become corrupted over time. Primal peoples understand this concept, and in order to maintain harmony they embed renewal and cleansing ceremonies in their systems,[12] whereas modern people have neglected to include such traditions.

One example of systemic corruption is the Bureau of Indian Affairs (B.I.A.), the government agency under the Department of Interior that is responsible for the welfare of Native Americans. The B.I.A. developed as an idea out of the old system of Indian Agents. These Indian Agents were often corrupt, cheating Indians out of their goods and supplies. President Ulysses S. Grant tried to root out the corruption of the Indian Agencies at one point by hiring known Christians from various denominations, especially Quakers. Grant was hoping to raise the level of morality in the Agency office. Eventually though, even with the inclusion of agents with higher moral fiber, the system returned to its former state of corruption.

---

12. According to our Cherokee traditional beliefs, it is the responsibility of human beings while they are on earth to maintain harmony and to restore harmony when it becomes broken. The Cherokee believe this is done primarily through keeping our traditional ceremonies. This understanding is similar to that of many other Native American tribal traditions.

For example, the agents once again began selling the beef and other supplies meant for the Indians, taking the profits for themselves, while whole reservations starved under their care. The system eventually became more bureaucratic, and today it is often referred to as one of the most obtuse and corrupted agencies in the U.S. system.

The B.I.A. (unaffectionately known among Native Americans as "Boss Indians Around") has, over its many years of serving as legal *en loco parentis* for Indians, stolen billons of dollars from *Individual Indian Money* accounts.[13] The old system of corruption did not even change when they began replacing white bureaucrats with Indian bureaucrats. As is always the case, the whole system took on a life of its own and became corrupt, regardless of who replaced whom.

The principle is plain. When we cease to trust the Creator for our daily provision, evil takes over and oppression occurs. Shalom, with its embedded concern for the poor, the marginalized, the animals, the birds, the earth, etcetera, is the divinely preferred way for humans to live. Justice and righteousness are weapons to be employed in order to combat evil, once the systems begin to become corrupted. Truth, which I will define here as following the natural paths of God's intentions, is also one of the main weapons that humans have been given in order to fight the temptation toward self-reliance.

Reliance on ourselves instead of the Creator can take the form of direct acts of selfishness or systems based on selfishness, but it can also develop by disregarding God's natural abundance on earth. Pollution of the earth, air, and water; species depletion; overuse of natural resources; genetically altered foods; foods infused with toxic chemicals — all are choices that bend toward a trajectory of human ingenuity over trusting God's provision. Conversely, shalom or the Native American Harmony Way reflects a worldview where life is understood in vital relationships based on familial reciprocity.

We Are All Related

The interconnection of all things as it is understood among the Plains Indians, especially among the Sioux Nations,[14] can be illustrated. While the

---

13. See *Cobell v. Salazar, Cobell v. Norton, Cobell v. Babbitt.*
14. The Dakota, Nakota, and Lakota tribes are commonly referred to as the "Sioux,"

same ideas are shared among most Native Americans, the Sioux concept
has become the most well known. Even though Sioux life was largely struc-
tured around warrior societies, there existed (and remains) a harmony way
as expressed through the interrelatedness of all things, including for them
the seven Sioux bands, other tribes, other humans, animals, birds, insects,
plants, and such. The Sioux concept that represents the acknowledgment
of this relationship is often expressed through the words of a common
prayer — *mitakuye oyasin.*

> A translation of *mitakuye oyasin* would better read: "For all the above
> me and below me and around me things." That is, for all my relations
> . . . it is this understanding of inter-relatedness, of balance and mutual
> respect of the different species in the world, that characterizes what we
> might call Indian people's greatest gift to Amer-Europeans and to the
> Amer-European understanding of creation at this time of world eco-
> logical crisis.[15]

The idea that all people and things are related to each other includes
all of humanity. This idea opens us to the possibility of once again becoming the family we already are. By realizing the connectedness of human-
kind to all animal life, we become aware of new possibilities for learning
and maintaining a concern for the preservation of all living things. A
worldview based on reciprocity and familial relatedness also has tremendous ecological implications. In humanity's dependence upon the earth,
we allow ourselves renewed opportunities for sustaining our planet and for
finding fresh prospects for developing food, water, and renewable energy.
All of this and more are contained in our simple prayers, in words like
mitakuye oyasin that describe the interrelatedness of all creation. Harmony
or balance is the key to all happiness, health, and well-being.

Among the Iroquoian peoples lived a Peacemaker who united five
Iroquoian tribes (with a sixth added later) during terrible times of war and
inner turmoil. The Six Nations still live according to the law and teachings
of the Peacemaker, whose view of harmonious living is consistent with
those already mentioned. *Tadodaho,* Chief Leon Shenandoah, comments,

---

an early misnomer that has survived and has now been incorporated into their own vocabulary. Because all three tribes or bands have a common spirituality, I refer to them all together
as Sioux.

15. Clara Sue Kidwell, Homer Noley, and George E. Tinker, *A Native American Theology* (Maryknoll, N.Y.: Orbis Books, 2003), 51.

The teachings are very good. The most important thing is that each individual must treat all others, all the people who walk on Mother Earth, including every nationality, with kindness. That covers a lot of ground. It doesn't apply only to my people. I must treat everyone I meet the same. When people turn their thoughts to the Creator, they give the Creator power to enter their minds and bring good thoughts. The most difficult part of this is that the Creator desired that there be no bloodshed among human beings and that there be peace, good relations, and always a good mind.[16]

Like the Lakota concept of *mitakuye oyasin,* the Iroquois construct of harmony seeks to bring all people together in one accord by recognizing that all people and creation are interconnected. In the following example, Chief Leon Shenandoah shares how this interconnectedness is related to the Harmony Way:

In explaining the good news to a chief named *Degaihogen, Degana-widah* presented a vision of a world community. "What shall we be like," *Degaihogen* had asked, "when this reason and righteousness and justice and health have come?" "In truth," replied *Deganawidah,* "reason brings righteousness, and reason is power that works among all minds alike. When once reason is established, all the minds of all mankind will be in a state of health and peace. It will be as if there were but a single person."[17]

The "reason" to which Chief Leon Shenandoah makes reference is the very relatedness of interconnectedness and living life in a harmonious existence. Many indigenous peoples share a common value of harmony as their preferred existence. A traditional Ojibwa Elder, Eddie Benton Banai,[18] writes, "Today, we should use these ancient teachings to live our lives in harmony with the plan that the Creator gave us. We are to do these things if we are to be natural people of the universe."[19] Benton Banai con-

16. Paul Wallace, *The Iroquois Book of Life: The White Roots of Peace* (Santa Fe, N.M.: Clear Light Publishing, 1994), 14.

17. Wallace, *The Iroquois Book of Life,* 108-9.

18. *Banai* is an honorary title bestowed upon traditional Ojibwa spiritual leaders. They are also referred to as *Gichi Dowin,* meaning "Big Medicine people."

19. Edward Benton Banai, *The Mishomis Book: The Voice of the Ojibway* (Hayward, Wisc.: Indian Country Communications, 1988), 9.

nects the past and the present through Harmony Way teachings, calling them "natural." He concludes his book by referring to the Ojibwa concept of harmony in their own language: "There are yet more teachings that can teach us how to live *ni-noo-do-da-di-win* (harmony) with the creation."[20] Whether exploring the Hebrew concept of shalom or the Native American Harmony Way as expressed among America's indigenes, a similar universal construct is at work for the good of all creation.

We Are All from One

In the following passage the apostle Paul seems to have been addressing universal human ontological issues from a perspective Native American people would recognize.

> "He is the God who made the world and everything in it. Since he is Lord of heaven and earth, he doesn't live in man-made temples, and human hands can't serve his needs — for he has no needs. He himself gives life and breath to everything, and he satisfies every need. From one man he created all the nations throughout the whole earth. He decided beforehand when they should rise and fall, and he determined their boundaries. His purpose was for the nations to seek after God and perhaps feel their way toward him and find him — though he is not far from any one of us. For in him we live and move and exist. As some of your own poets have said, 'We are his offspring.' And since this is true, we shouldn't think of God as an idol designed by craftsmen from gold or silver or stone." (Acts 17:24-29 NLT)

First the apostle says, "He is the God who made the world and everything in it," making it clear that he is referring to the Creator of everything. Traditional Native North American belief is, by and large, monotheistic. I have heard it said often among Native Americans, "You can pray with anyone, since there is only one God who hears us all." Next, Paul points out that "human hands can't serve his needs," showing that the Creator is too great to be held in human control. This portion is reminiscent of Isaiah 66:1, "This is what the LORD says: Heaven is my throne, and the earth is my footstool. Could you build me a temple as good as that? Could you build

20. Banai, *The Mishomis Book,* 113.

me such a resting place?" Isaiah is presenting a rhetorical question. The obvious answer is "no," God cannot be contained by human-made earthly temples. Neither can he be contained in human ingenuity. But the good creation itself, made by the Creator, "God's throne," reminds us that God is eternal. The next sentence, "He himself gives life and breath to everything, and he satisfies every need," reminds us that true security rests in trusting the Creator and the abundance that God supplies.

"From one man," Paul continues, "he created all the nations throughout the whole earth." The Hebrew story of *Adam* fulfills Paul's idea of "one man." Here, Paul concludes that from Adam, our common ancestor, God made every *ethnē* (ethnic group). The theological implications necessitate a discussion on the inherent goodness of cultural diversity.

> Each people group possesses unique understanding and giftings that God has placed within that culture. Someone has said, "The whole counsel of God is found in the whole Body of Christ." But each people group also wears cultural blinders. No individual alone, and no people group alone, can fully understand God. But working together, uniting our many different experiences, cultures, and understandings, we can see more of the greatness of God. This concept can be threatening to those who feel they need to control things and who must maintain a rigorous superiority to others. Yet I am pretty sure that God can handle all this diversity, and that He enjoys the many and varying ways we relate to Him and express our devotion. Just as no one person has a "universal" voice pattern, retinal design or set of fingerprints, no one culture has the "correct" view of God. Since the Creator has gone to great lengths to create and establish a distinct "DNA pattern" for every culture throughout the world, with no two identical, shouldn't we in the Church set about the task of finding out why this diversity is so precious to the heart of God?[21]

When we ignore the truth found in the natural order of diversity, it must greatly disappoint the Creator. After all, we are God's art. As Paul says in Ephesians 2:10a, "we are his workmanship." The New Living Translation states, "we are God's masterpiece." Fine paintings usually reflect a variety of colors, hues, shades, and textures. Can you imagine rejecting

---

21. Randy Woodley, *Living in Color: Embracing God's Passion for Ethnic Diversity* (Downers Grove, Ill.: InterVarsity, 2001), 29-30.

such a masterpiece because it was not all in a single color? In essence, to reject the beauty of natural diversity is to reject the Master Artist himself. Through God's injunction to humans and to the rest of creation to "fill the earth," the wise Creator set the canvas. God knew that as his created beings (human and nonhuman) spread across the earth, they would for a time become isolated from one another. Therefore, each distinctive genetic pool that isolation produced — each unique language, the individual food traditions, the music, art, religious ceremony — was just another stroke laid to the canvas from the brush of the Master Artist. The differences were good from the beginning, and they are still good today!

Recent genetic studies have borne similar findings. Discoveries made by Dr. Spencer Wells and the Genographic Project have found a corollary to Paul's observation, but genetic science refers to the first humans as "Scientific Adam" and "Scientific Eve." By tracing our genetic markers, the latest genetic findings posit that all human beings are related because we all share a common ancestor. The Genographic Project claims that genetically all humans are a 99.9 percent match.[22] Fortunately, the 0.1 percent difference enables science to trace us to our common ancestors. Perhaps this new research will give us pause if we can realize that whenever we act out of character from shalom, we are hurting our own family members.

As human beings pushed toward the boundaries of their new homes ("he determined their boundaries"), they were able to understand things about God from a variety of perspectives: "His purpose was for the nations to seek after God and perhaps feel their way toward him and find him." The apostle Paul reminds us, "[H]e is not far from any one of us. For in him we live and move and exist." Indeed, God is not far away but ever so near. We are reminded of God's closeness through his creativity when we appreciate the variety of cultures and human physical traits.

The intention of diversity in our various relationships must also take into account how we are related to nonhuman creation. The diversity found in nonhuman creation and the many varieties of reciprocal relationships teach us how much we all are meant to depend on each other in loving relationship. They are a sign that the God who loves interconnected community is among us. We are all familiar with the statistic that humans share 98.5 percent of our DNA with a chimpanzee — but we also share

---

22. https://genographic.nationalgeographic.com/genographic/index.html, last accessed on May 31, 2011.

40 percent of our DNA with a simple daffodil.[23] Whether one believes that these relationships are from an evolutionary connection or that the Creator used much of the same materials in our construction, or both, we cannot escape the fact that we are all somehow related.

If we think of waging war against other human beings, we should first admit that they are our own distant brothers, sisters, aunts, uncles and grandparents, children and grandchildren. If we continue wantonly extracting the earth's resources, we should admit that she is our mother and all the other species on which we share the planet are our relatives. Finally, we people who are "walking earth" should face the fact that we cannot continue on these destructive paths without hurting ourselves and our future generations. We are truly all related.

We Are All One with Each Other

Another model of relatedness reflects research from the revolutionary science of quantum physics:

> In its exploration of the physical world science has increasingly found that concepts of atomism and mechanism, useful as they undoubtedly are for some purposes, are nevertheless unable to express fully the character of physical reality. . . . The history of twentieth-century physics can be read as the story of the discovery of many levels of intrinsic relationality present in the structure of the universe.[24]

How does the Creator design the universe? Note the phrase "many levels of intrinsic relationality present in the structure of the universe." Regardless of our differences, as wonderful as they are, we are all in this thing together. I remember a line from an old gospel song, "wrapped up, tied up, tangled all up in Jesus." Acknowledging that Christ is the Creator, this line is truer than the one who first penned it suspected. *Quantum entanglement,* one of the many suppositions of quantum physics, concerns itself with physical relationality at a subatomic level. Quantum entanglement

23. The relationship is evident regardless of whether or not one has evolutionist or creationist assumptions, and it does not prove or disprove either assumption. See http://personal.uncc.edu/jmarks/interests/aaa/marksaaa99.htm, last accessed on May 31, 2011.

24. John Polkinghorne, ed., *The Trinity and an Entangled World: Relationality in Physical Science and Theology* (Grand Rapids: Eerdmans, 2010), vii.

demonstrates that we share breath and matter with everything and everyone around us. The closer we move to something or someone, the more that entity becomes a part of us. The longer we maintain our proximity to someone or something, the more we share each other. In a real, scientifically verifiable, subatomic sense, no one actually ends where their skin stops. In fact, quite the opposite is true. We are a part of everything around us and everything around us is a part of us. What a magnificent design to ponder! "Stick with me" while we explore this together (pun intended).

When juxtaposing new findings from the field of quantum physics and from our understanding of shalom/Native American Harmony Way, new theological perspectives are opened to us. For example, consider the metaphor of us all being Christ's body — it becomes more literal than we might care to admit. When we are all together in one room, we are sharing more than a metaphor. And this is as it should be according to Colossians 1:17b, referring to Christ: "[H]e holds all creation together" (NLT).

Even as you read this I bet your mind is taking this information and going straight to the part of your brain that classifies these things as metaphor. I know, because it is what I am tempted to do. But somehow, let's pull the information back out of the metaphor box and think a bit longer on the physical reality. Christ, the Creator, from the community of Trinity, designs and creates everything from similar "stuff." At least part of that "stuff" we have discovered, is what we are calling DNA — the basic building material of life (although to God our discoveries are probably more like watching children play in a sandbox). Not only does Christ create all things, but he holds all things together, literally. Perhaps this shouldn't surprise us. Even the Greek poem quoted by Paul in Acts 17:28 (NLT) reveals the greater truth, "For in him we live and move and exist. As some of your own poets have said, 'We are his offspring.'" We should contemplate the implications of such deep concerns. Maybe a simple symbol can help.

Lessons from the Sacred Circle

Another model for understanding harmony and our relationship to everything is a simple symbol among Native Americans — the circle. The interconnectedness within the Harmony Way is most often referred to symbolically as a circle or a hoop. Among Native Americans the Harmony Way is not a philosophy; it is a whole way of being and doing life. To Euro-westerners, a philosophy is something that can simply be believed, but the

Harmony Way, like shalom, is tangible. Living out the Harmony Way requires not only a belief, but also action, which aligns itself in participation with the whole of the universe. The circle is the tangible symbol that represents this understanding.

Canadian Cree theologian Stan McKay draws the harmony connection to the Sacred Circle and the respect present among our aboriginal peoples:

> The image of living on the earth in harmony with creation and therefore the Creator, is a helpful image for me. . . . Each day we are given is for thanksgiving for the earth. We are to enjoy it and share it in service of others. This is the way to grow in unity and harmony. . . . It allows for diversity within the unity of the Creator. . . . There are many teachings in the aboriginal North American Nations that use the symbol of the circle. It is the symbol for the inclusive caring community, where individuals are respected and interdependence is recognized. In the wider perspective it symbolizes the natural order of creation in which human beings are part of the whole circle of life. Aboriginal spiritual teachers speak of the re-establishment of the balance between human beings and the whole of creation, as a mending of the hoop.[25]

My friend the Reverend Fern Cloud, whose ministry is called "Healing the Hoop," makes a distinction between the tendency of a more western worldview to see the Harmony Way as a philosophy: "*Wo 'dakota* (the Dakota understanding of harmony) is not a philosophy, it's a path of life we do, looking at what Creator gave us, in that whole circle of life, and living it." To Cloud and to many Native Americans, this point is crucial.

The circle or hoop as a symbol of life is found in nearly all Native North American tribes. The symbol is a powerful representation of the earth, life, seasons, cycles of maturity, etcetera. The symbolism of the circle is one of the oldest in North America, having been found in various parts of the country in ancient petroglyphs. It is included in Native American traditions. Many of the ceremonies, such as Sundance, Powwow, Native American Church, and Ghost Dance, are fashioned intentionally in a circle. In observing the outdoors you will find that a circle is a common and natural shape. Trees, rocks, whirlpools, tornadoes, flowers, etcetera all

---

25. James Treat, *Native and Christian: Indigenous Voices on Religious Identity in the United States and Canada* (New York: Routledge, 1996), 54-55.

bear a common resemblance to circular objects rather than triangles or squares. In general, right angles do not naturally occur in nature without assistance from human beings.

The circle represents to many North American indigenous peoples a sense of harmony and wholeness. The list of tribes whose overall life-ways promote a similar view of harmony could possibly include every North American Native tribal group. Tangibly, the symbolism of the circle and its related ideas is evidenced in Native North America by a common spirituality, often expressed by other common symbols including eagle feathers, and in burning medicine plants (i.e., sage, sweetgrass, cedar). Even beyond common symbols, there is much in common spiritually among America's First Peoples, including the reality of disharmony. While there are likely more stories of how disharmony came into the world than there are tribes, I will share one story from my own tribal people.

Disharmony Resulting in Ill Health

The following is my own recollection of the Cherokee story of how disease came into the world. This story varies slightly depending on who is telling it, but I will share it as it was told to me by a traditional Cherokee friend. The story tells us that disease came upon our people because we grew out of harmony with the animals, not giving thanks for the gift of food we were given. I share the story in an abbreviated form and hope that it still reveals an important point, namely, that the origin of human disease and suffering is attributed to broken harmony in creation.

> Every traditional Cherokee knows that it is considered polite to thank the Creator and the animal when it furnishes its own life so people may eat and sustain their lives. It was said that during this "era of ingratitude" the Cherokees even began to kill that which they were not going to eat. These were evil days indeed!
>
> As a result of these abuses, the animals held council, in order to protect themselves from the evil that had come upon the once grateful Cherokee. After much debate, the animals decided to bring diseases upon the Cherokee people. The Cherokees began getting sick and dying from these diseases. After many Cherokees had died they pleaded with the animals, "Please, we will become grateful and kill only that which we will eat." But the animals would not recant.

At the same time, the plants were watching all of these things. They watched as the Cherokee children got sick, and even died. The plants decided to hold a council. In the council they agreed to provide medicine for the Cherokee. Each night, as the Cherokees would sleep, the plants would come to them in their dreams and show them how to use the plants to heal the diseases that the animals had brought upon them.

The Cherokees recovered and agreed to kill only what they absolutely needed. They also agreed to say a prayer of thanks to any animal that they killed, and to any plant that would be harvested for food or medicine. The Creator was happy with the Cherokees once again because harmony was restored among all that he had created.

The story asserts a holistic view of relationships. Harmony was broken between human beings, the Creator, and the animals through ingratitude. The ingratitude was expressed in two ways — not giving thanks, and killing what was not to be eaten — both of which are an affront to God and the natural order of creation. Disease and death came into the world through animals (creation). The healing also came through the creation (plants). Humans were restored back to the creation and as a result, back to God.[26]

One of the points often made after this story is told is that for every disease spread to humans by animals, there is a plant that can cure it. This very much involves balance, restoration, and harmony between the Creator and all creation. It depicts a time of broken harmony, but through the mending of the hoop all is restored to the way Creator intended it to be. In Cherokee thinking, restoration must include restoring the larger holistic relationship between Creator, human beings, and the rest of creation. Only when the whole of creation is restored can there be harmony.

The story also teaches us to be grateful for everything we have. One expression of this gratefulness means that we kill only that which we are going to eat. My Ojibwa friend and elder, Dave Soney, once told me about a time when he was ten years old and he killed a robin. His mother made him clean it, cook it, and eat it to demonstrate a similar lesson. Gratitude among our Indian people is extremely important and considered to be an important part of living in harmony. Among many indigenous people,

---

26. Cherokee ceremonies most often involve earthly symbols to express restoration and harmony.

most morning ceremonies begin with a thanksgiving ceremony of some kind. The custodial relationship we have with the earth and that the earth has with us is expressed as gratitude in all that we do. If we are not grateful, we cannot live out the Harmony Way and we become sick people.

This principle is also illustrated in the well-known Iroquois story of the Peacemaker. In the story, a man named Hiawatha was grief-stricken at the loss of his six daughters who died as a result of inner tribal warring. A shaman, the Great Cannibal, who lived in the woods by himself, eventually caused the death of Hiawatha's youngest and remaining daughter. At her death, Hiawatha went mad. It is said that at the time before the Great Peacemaker there was actual cannibalism among the people. People's inner pain and imbalance had caused them to act in ways inconsistent with the principles of harmony the Peacemaker would bring. The conclusion of the story is that Hiawatha was consoled, and the Peacemaker, with the help of Hiawatha, was able to bring restoration and balance to those warring nations.

Among Native Americans there is no physical and emotional/spiritual dichotomy. Traditionally, when a person is physically ill, a reputable healer will often go to that person's home to get a fuller picture of what is occurring in the sick person's life. The medicine person asks not only about the symptoms but also about dreams, feelings, and strains in relationships that have occurred lately in that person's life. In addition, medicine given to a patient is always accompanied by prayer.

Working Through the Pain of Disharmony

Native Americans, with the worst health-related demographics in the nation, understand these problems to be brought on by the disharmonious effects of colonization. The following quote by John Mohawk concerning the health risks of colonization upon Native Americans and our values bears examination.

> Colonization is the greatest health risk to indigenous peoples as individuals and communities. It produces the anomie — the absence of values and sense of group purpose and identity — that underlies the deadly automobile accidents triggered by alcohol abuse. It creates the conditions of inappropriate diet which lead to an epidemic of degenerative diseases, and the moral anarchy that leads to child abuse and

spousal abuse. Becoming colonized was the worst thing that could happen five centuries ago, and being colonized is the worst thing that can happen now.[27]

Mohawk draws a direct line from colonization to the everyday ills among Native Americans. If Mohawk is correct in naming colonization as one of the greatest health risks to Native Americans (and I believe he is), then colonization is, in a real sense, a sickness from which Native Americans and others must be delivered and healed. According to Mohawk, the path to better health, wellness, or well-being for Native Americans is de-colonization. But decolonization in and of itself is incomplete because it fails to remove the systemic relationships embedded in colonialism and neocolonialism.

My intention in discussing American colonial history is neither to blame the oppressor nor to excuse the victim.[28] As an oppressed minority, Native Americans understand well the facts of victimization through colonization and the reality of continual victimization through the present neocolonial system, but as oppressed people, we are not without agency. By finding solutions to our own problems, we do not remain helpless victims waiting to be assimilated into the values of the dominant society.

The unfortunate history of this continent is that American and Canadian colonial national constructions have molded Native Americans into a deep and unhealthy dependency through offering *their* solutions to *our* problems. These presumed solutions have taken the form of organization and reorganization of tribal governments, ethnic status categories, government grants, health service, welfare, and education, just to name a few. This dependency by design has stripped Native people of our dignity. The consequences of this dependent system are catastrophic. As a result, harmony has been severely broken. However, all is not lost. In this process I am reminded of the words of Albert Memmi: "The decolonized find fault in everyone but themselves: It is the fault of history, or of whites, but as long as the decolonized do not free themselves from such

---

27. John C. Mohawk, "The Tragedy of Colonization," *Indian Country Today*, January 23, 2004. http://www.indiancountrytoday.com/archive/28212749.html, accessed January 15, 2010.

28. Several decades ago the social sciences focused on the dilemma of the victim. While much truth can be found in understanding the victim, this critique left a gap in the ability of the victim to find power or agency to resist victimization. Social scientists have now moved beyond victimization to seeing people as agents of change in their own right.

evasions they will be unable to correctly analyze their conditions and act accordingly."[29]

These "evasions" are interpreted by Memmi to mean exaggerated pain. While one is hardly able to exaggerate the pain in Native America, Memmi is correct in the sense that pain is freeing when it serves as a catalyst either to the colonized or the colonizers. When colonizers are confronted rightly with their egregious inhumanity, the pain is shared and doubled. In an instant, this pain naturally transforms itself into guilt. Both the pain of the colonized and the guilt of the colonizers can easily become retreats of inaction. Yet by acknowledging the source of our own pain, we are not retreating but are taking a step toward right action. This is the tough work of restoring harmony to the present society in which we now live.

Educators Myles Horton and Paulo Freire collaborated in a book where their dialogue was recorded. Freire addresses the posture of the effective educator by stating that "conflicts are the midwife of consciousness."[30] If this is true, then perhaps great acts of harmony may be born out of such great pain. When speaking of Native American identity, the reality of internal conflict is presupposed, but sometimes it is more difficult for members of the dominant society to recognize where the problems lie. In order to identify the causes of disharmony, it is necessary to juxtapose common Euro-western ideas with commonly held Native American understandings.

All peoples are influenced by their social history. No one people group wins the prize for best society, but some are worse than others. When the Europeans arrived in our country, most did not care to understand the value of our past. Conversely, Native Americans have been forced to learn the history and societal concerns of Euro-America. We have had the time to critique it and make suggestions on improving life. Perhaps the time has come for our people groups to find the best in one another, and at the same time heal ourselves and the earth in the process.

---

29. Albert Memmi, *Colonization and the Colonized* (Boston: Beacon Press, 1991), 19.

30. Brenda Bell, John Gaventa, and John Peters, *We Make the Road by Walking: Conversations on Education and Social Change with Paulo Freire and Myles Horton* (Philadelphia: Temple University Press, 1990), 187.

CHAPTER FIVE

The Great Thinking/Doing Divide

Cogito Ergo Sum

René Descartes, the seventeenth-century French philosopher who penned the above words — meaning "I think, therefore I am" — is sometimes referred to as the father of modern philosophy. Descartes' influence was both profound and reflective of his times. One of his contributions to modernity was to help set the stage for the human mind to be understood as the primary function of all human beings. In this sense, he resurrected old dualistic paradigms that resulted in placing the mind and body in separate spheres of reality. Descartes' form of dualism, like other similar historical forms of dualism, gave permission for the rational mind to trump physical or experiential realities. In the sphere of creation, Descartes contributed to modern dualistic notions of separation between humans and animals, the latter of which he presumed not to have a soul. Descartes can also be credited for modern understandings of mechanisms that likely contributed to the rise of industrialization.

In his efforts to create philosophical categories, Descartes popularized the vivisection of animals and human corpses for scientific research. Whether Descartes' actions of dissecting human and animal corpses influenced his philosophy or his philosophy justified his actions is not altogether clear. What is clear is that they are related. Descartes was by no means the first one in history to fail to recognize the sacredness of the whole human person or the sacredness of animals, but his actions, and the influence of other rationalists, had considerable sway on the modern, western worldview, even until today.

It is a little-known story, but for over a century the United States War Department assisted in conducting scientific research on Native Americans. During the "Indian Wars," especially after battles, officials from the army, medical doctors, scientists, anthropologists, etcetera would remove various body parts of fallen Native Americans or even confiscate the entire body. The bodies and body parts were then shipped to places such as the Smithsonian in Washington, D.C., to be studied. Often, these "specimens" ended up being displayed at curios stores or as specimens in museums. The "scientific" studies often focused on the Native American cranium, and as a result, many of the body parts abducted were therefore human heads.

With the advent in 1990 of NAGPRA (Native American Graves Protection and Repatriation Act), a commission was established to investigate these and other claims of atrocities. Since many of the Native American bodies and body parts were marked with their location of origin, and/or tribal identity, a comprehensive plan was set in place to return the marked remains to their respective tribes. In fact, this process has already begun.

Although a complete investigation is still ongoing, it has already been established that an estimated 100,000 plus human, Native American remains are still listed as "culturally unidentifiable." In other words, someone forgot to mark the original box, or perhaps a marker tag was lost over the years. Native Americans feel it is paramount that the unidentifiable remains of our ancestors are returned to a place of permanent rest in an honorable way.[1]

To Native Americans, the sorts of actions that occurred in the name of science are reprehensible. A corpse, according to our Indian ways, should be treated as sacred, with respect and with ceremony. Viewed through a Native American worldview, the actions of those who were abducting our ancestors' flesh and bones are horrifying. Having come through the Enlightenment, with the philosophical influence of Descartes and others, those actions made perfect sense to the people who thought they were forwarding the cause of science.

1. See the efforts of the National Friends Service Committee, http://www.fcnl.org/issues/item.php?item_id=1470&issue_id=96, last accessed January 10, 2010.

Educating for Shalom

As a professional educator, I have noticed a pattern in Euro-western think-ing. The learning style of Americans is often very different from the learn-ing styles of many Native Americans.[2] Often western religion is expressed in *beliefs*. To Native Americans, *practices* are beliefs. In other words, one comes to believe something because one does it.[3] The dominant Euro-western American learning system seems primarily to be concerned with verifiable facts, which they call "knowledge."

In much of the modern American educational system, students are taught to absorb data through memorization — one concept being built upon another. The data itself is seen to have no moral value, being viewed as mere facts. Knowledge, in this system, is measured by standardized tests and grades, causing students to believe that their lives are fundamentally in competition with others. The Euro-western American system is de-signed by white Americans, for white American students, who come from a particular Euro-western worldview.

The emphasis on experience comes much later in the education of a student in the American educational process (often considered to be the expertise stage), when integrative skills are encouraged that set the student apart from those who have either not mastered as many facts, or those who have not integrated those facts as well as others, or possibly both. In this model of education, knowledge is "sold" by the school, "purchased," and eventually "owned" by the student. What the student does in the integra-tive stage will determine whether or not its use is employed as wise or moral actions. All along, the system has been taught within a highly struc-tured atmosphere of compartmentalized learning modules. The system re-

2. I believe colloquialisms such as "Education for all," "Education is everyone's right," and "We can only better ourselves through education" are all Trojan horses that are used to assuage our Native American sensibilities and invite us to lose ourselves in the system. Na-tive Americans should not uncritically enter in the academy without admitting that, when we do, we have already compromised a part of our indigenous well-being. The modern west-ern educational system is built on thin ice and at any moment the ice may break and we can be swallowed by its icy depths. Obviously, due to colonization, the ice has been broken and we lack good models. Our Native educational institutions generally reflect the same patterns as seen in the Euro-American society and church. There is a need for better models.

3. This is not always true. An example of a Euro-western thinker promoting similar constructs can be found in George Lindbeck, *The Nature of Doctrine: Religion and Theology in a Postliberal Age* (Philadelphia: Westminster, 1984), 64. In it, the theologian argues that doctrinal theology is much more holistic than a set of cognitive propositions.

sults are conclusive, and produce competitive, capitalistic, individualistic, extrinsic categorically oriented, relationally disconnected thinkers who understand themselves to be in a "morally neutral" role. This "morally neutral" role is seen as a powerful state of moral high ground.[4] Furthermore, the system teaches students that life should be viewed as foundationally compartmentalized through a type of *pseudo-time,* as opposed to natural time.[5]

Coupled with the western myth of historical progress, western influences such as Augustine's just war theory, and the Calvinistic myth of divine blessing, the Euro-western educational process sets up wealthy white Americans (and those from other races who "buy" into the system) to believe that in some very tangible ways they can and should exert their power over others. In other words, the unspoken values that are taught within the modern American education system are influential in leading those in power to believe that they deserve to rule the world by the spread of their ideals. In the case of the United States, these ideals are spread primarily through military subjugation, in the name of democracy and capitalism.[6]

Traditional Native American ways of learning are taught on a different basis, which I believe to be more closely aligned with the principles of shalom.

Among Native Americans, knowledge is essentially experiential and it is integrated with morality and wisdom. Instead of knowledge being viewed as private and protected, it is viewed more as community property,

---

4. Author Jerry Mander confesses, "Our assumption of superiority does not come to us by accident. We have been trained in it. It is soaked into the fabric of Western religion, economic systems and technology. They reek of their greater virtues and capabilities." Jerry Mander, *In the Absence of the Sacred: The Failure of Technology and the Survival of the Indian Nations* (San Francisco: Sierra Club Books, 1992), 209. Contemporary practitioners may be tempted to view themselves as immune from the sense of entitlement and superiority that their historical counterparts exhibited. People tend to look at the past as moving from less civilized to more civilized, especially if they are the ones writing the new history.

5. These concepts of time will be explained in the following chapter.

6. The U.S. military is in 150 countries around the world (see Dept. of Defense Statistics, http://siadapp.dmdc.osd.mil/personnel/MILITARY/history/hst0712.pdf). America has been directly responsible for overthrowing at least fourteen sovereign governments in order to gain influence and extract the wealth of these nations. See Stephen Kinzer's *Overthrow: America's Century of Regime Change from Hawaii to Iraq* (New York: Times Books, 2006). Most of these actions are justified under the myth of the spreading of democracy. Note also the history of United States involvement in the World Bank and the International Monetary Fund.

usually kept or "stewarded" by elders or wisdom keepers. To indigenous Americans, knowledge is not abstract or neutral; it is directly related to life experience, stories, songs, ceremonies, and traditions. Native Americans do not categorize knowledge extrinsically but according to relational categories in the natural world.

Among indigenous people, integration of the "data" is continually occurring, especially as related to other contexts like spirituality, family, and society. In addition, for Native Americans, the character of the teacher and the relationship between the student and the teacher are at least as important as the content. Among Native Americans, real learning seems to happen more naturally, and knowledge is held by and for the good of the community, not for individual advancement or benefit.

The differences between Native American and the dominant Euro-western American cultural forms of education are apparent.

> In the Native worldview a person who knows mostly theory is considered to know very little; and most of what means something to American Indians cannot be learned in books. What is more important to a group of Native Americans? Honesty, wisdom and experience. In Indian country true knowledge is not so much about facts as it is revelation from God. I was taught by elders to observe closely when a task was being done and not to ask questions. After awhile I was given the opportunity to try it, and I was corrected when I messed up. I was told to pray about these things and meditate on them. Every so often my questions — which were still in my heart and mind — would be answered. This learning style was very different from my training in college and seminary, where I was certified based on my knowledge of certain facts. In the Indian world we *experience;* in the Euro-American world we *gather facts* about it. Someone has said that Native Americans would rather participate in a ceremony while Euro-Americans would generally rather read a book about it.[7]

Traditional Native American education is designed to produce fundamental cooperation among the group — group cohesion, sharing of knowledge and resources, respect for those with more experience, respect for the community, respect for diversity, a fundamental sense of relatedness, and a

7. Randy Woodley, *Living in Color: Embracing God's Passion for Ethnic Diversity* (Downers Grove, Ill.: InterVarsity, 2001), 48-49.

sense of humility. My observations and assumptions concerning Euro-American learning styles may be offensive to some people, especially those who have bought into the dominant American education model. If so, I apologize. It is not my intention to offend but merely to suggest that there are reasons why the current systems exist. Perhaps if we can understand those reasons better, we can all benefit by changing the current system.

I came to these observations by having been a recipient of both the Euro-western and indigenous educational models. I also noticed a particular commonality among those from a western worldview when it came to participating in and observing Native American ceremonies. Those from the western paradigm are taught to critically examine everything. They seek to find the meaning and the history behind every symbol before the ceremony begins or else they are reluctant to participate. Some of their concerns are unfounded and fear-based, but I found that there is something more to the questions about our ceremonies than fear of idolatry or fear of syncretism.

I have been leading Sweat lodges since 1990.[8] Over the years I have observed, in Sweat and other ceremonies, that white folks ask many questions prior to a ceremony. Some of the questions I have been asked about Sweat include: How many rocks are used? What is the history of Sweat lodge? How long have I been running the Sweat? What temperature will it be? What is the meaning of the smoke? Etcetera. When I first began leading Sweat and non-Indians asked these questions, I usually answered them even though I felt uneasy about it. I also noticed that American Indians never asked about these things. Then one day I overheard one of the white guys who had been in Sweat lodge with us in the past, explaining the ceremony to another white guy who was coming in for the first time. It was apparent that the guy with only two Sweat lodge experiences thought of himself as an expert on Indian Sweat lodge. This should have been no surprise to me, since in his own educational system his expertise was based on knowledge, not experience.

Over the years I have noticed that non-Indians, from a western-oriented educational system, want to know all the facts. When they have

8. A Sweat lodge is a conical sauna-type construction, made of willows and canvas. Rocks are heated outside in a fire and brought into the structure. Water is poured on the rocks and people pray, sing, and share in a particular order. Native Americans sometimes refer to the Sweat as America's first church since it has been practiced for centuries, perhaps millennia. Indeed, certain permissions and training are needed to run a public Sweat ceremony. I sometimes refer to the Sweat lodge as a combination between a Wednesday evening prayer meeting and a Swedish sauna.

memorized the facts, or attained adequate knowledge of the subject at hand, they naturally feel as though they have expertise in the matter. It does not matter to them that they have never been trained to actually *do* the task at hand; it only matters that they have more knowledge of it than the person to whom they are explaining it. Sadly for them, I also noticed that by "dissecting" the ceremony, much of the sacredness and beauty was lost.

I discovered early on that the best way to help a non-Indian to enjoy a Sweat lodge ceremony was to tell them that I would answer any questions they have, but not until we sat down to share a meal after the ceremony is completed. Often, non-Indians will comment that the Sweat lodge, done in this way, was one of the most spiritual experiences they had ever had. In this way I have been able to share the beauty and mystery of one of our ceremonies in a way that seems to change people's lives.

To know is more than a cognitive exercise. As with anything, when we think about the Creator, there is mystery involved. Part of human spirituality is to be content to leave the mystery as mystery. Knowing about something or someone (a person, a fact, a shape, or an equation) is only a thin slice of the feast available that a fuller sense of knowledge has to offer us. As whole human beings our reality includes every part of us, and it includes the whole context of the world around us. We feel, we see, we touch, we taste, we hear, and we sense intuitively the world around us. How is it that we are willing to settle for one anemic part of the full spectrum of knowledge, that which we can cognitively know? I would answer by stating emphatically that in some very real ways, the west has traded its humanity for power.

The quest for power (that which is derived from imagined superiority because of having certain kinds of knowledge) has allowed the west to buy into an educational system based on only a few realities. Knowledge, in the western system, has been parsed and split into acceptable categories, removed from the whole of reality. Learning and filling in these categories gets the seeker the rewards of the system. In the process, teaching others what is important to the system ends up being all that is important in the system. The system is fundamentally flawed and needs an overhaul.

The Vicious Idea

What shaped Europe into designing an educational approach that views a reality that is largely without essence? The nations of western Europe, meaning primarily in this case England, Spain, France, Portugal, Germany,

Belgium, Holland, and later America, desired to be on the cutting edge of economic expansion at various times during the sixteenth to nineteenth centuries. As great colonial powers, these nations were competing to become empires of wealth. Because they had developed particular technologies, especially concerning weaponry (accompanied by justifiable attitudes toward killing), they did what the rich and powerful often do. The intoxication of their own ideas allowed them to fool themselves into believing that they were not just wealthy and powerful, but also smart and wise.

During this time, the western European nations developed a philosophy and a pedagogy that would undergird their exploitations and justify their cruelties. They created systematic ways of believing their own false assumptions. They most often justified their false philosophical assumptions by calling them civilized and even Christian (notions that were often seen as parallel). The presumed height of this era was called the "Enlightenment" or the "Age of Reason." The colonizing countries of western Europe were the main benefactors of the Enlightenment-bound Euro-western worldview.

America, not to be left out, was born in this toxic atmosphere. Americans drank from the same cup of power as the Europeans. Like the rest of the "civilized world" in search of new worlds to conquer, Americans filled their cups, perhaps even more than any others, and became drunk with all the false assumptions necessary to perfect Enlightenment ideas with the exploits of colonialism. What were the false assumptions handed down from the Enlightenment?

Principally, these philosophical errors had to do with dualistic perceptions of reality. To understand this question better it may be helpful to travel back in time, even farther than the "Age of Reason" in western Europe. European and American forms of dualism have their roots all the way back to ancient Greece. What is dualism? Dualism, in its basic form, is a way of perceiving reality within a framework of two opposing rudiments such as spirit and flesh, mind and body, mind and matter, or good and evil.

Dualism is a broad subject and is by no means isolated to Europeans. It shows up on history's radar long before ancient Greece. Some would argue that the church has spent a great deal of time and energy rooting out dualistic heresies and therefore cannot be dualistic. I would argue that dualism was ubiquitous to the church, and like the nose on one's own face, dualism was easier to see on someone else's face than our own. One way to understand a concept is to contrast it with the opposite category. In this sense, dualism's opposite is holism. I have been arguing that both ancient

Semitic worldviews and the basic worldview of indigenous people are holistic and therefore, fundamentally fitted to embrace shalom. As explained earlier, shalom is a holistic concept. A worldview influenced by shalom would in many ways be the opposite of a worldview influenced by dualism.

In a holistic worldview, all of creation (the material world) is considered both good and spiritual. In a dualistic worldview, only the spirit is considered to be good; creation (the material world, including our own body) is considered to be either evil or less spiritual. In Christianity we can easily view the departure from a holistic worldview by discussing the "soul." We speak of Jesus "saving our souls"; reaching "souls for Christ," and our "souls going to heaven." Most often, the way these terms are used is a departure from biblical Christianity. In Scripture, Jesus "saves" (the Greek word *sōzō*, meaning to heal or to make whole) our whole person.

Our salvation (or healing) implies the restoration of our whole selves to God and the whole of creation, including our social and physical selves. The biblical injunction for evangelism is not to get people's souls to heaven but rather to introduce them to the renewed community of creation through Christ. In Scripture our souls do not depart from our bodies. The resurrection of the dead is a bodily resurrection. The biblical composite is not about God's interest in our soul or spirit; it is one where God is interested in our viewing all of creation as having spiritual qualities.

The kind of dualism I am referring to also provided the basis for a philosophical split in understanding reality. Dividing reality into categories can be a useful tool if we do not attempt to treat the categories as if they are the whole of reality. Unfortunately, in the Euro-western worldview, the categories themselves are often seen as the whole truth rather than being seen in the context of their wholeness. Extrinsic categorization, which divided the theoretical part from the practical whole, has created civilizations that attempt to live life out in mere fragments of reality.

Modern theological dualism began at the University of Berlin with the work of Friedrich Schleiermacher. Ever since then, the American academy and the American church have fed at the trough of modern dualism, dividing reality between the practical and theoretical. Western Enlightenment influences dichotomized the world (including the philosophical and theological realms) by separating humanity from nature and then dividing those partial realities into extrinsic categories. It is this reality that allows western Christians to easily ignore their responsibility to care for the earth. This type of dualism eventually led to a Christianity that promoted the split between theory and practice. Academically, it actually takes on a form of classism that appears as the theoretical (that which is primarily for scholars) and the practical (regular cognition open for everyone).

The problem with such a division of reality was that false dichotomies in reality, when believed, take on a life of their own by creating their own momentum. The western world soon found itself living into the extrinsic categories of reality that it had created. Western Christians, whose roots come from a fundamentally holistic religion, also found themselves developing a worldview with a divided reality.[9]

For example, prior to the Enlightenment, Christian mission was considered the "mother of theology,"[10] but after the Enlightenment influence, what Christians believed and what they actually did could be understood separately. In other words, it was now possible that one could hold correct doctrinal beliefs and not demonstrate them, and even act contrary to those beliefs. After the categories were created, people only needed a rationale to tip the scales in favor of orthodoxy (correct beliefs) over orthopraxis (correct action). In such a categorically ordered worldview it was possible to justify one's Christian faith with actions deemed contrary to Christianity, as long as one held correct doctrine.

A host of problems resulted in false dichotomization because reality does not divide well for long. Once "practical theology" could be placed into its own category, it left room for the creation of the idea of a "nonpractical theology." This unnatural divide lent itself to the old dualistic system of the material world versus the spiritual world. As mentioned earlier, a dualistic worldview is nearly the polar opposite of a harmony worldview. This meant trouble for the indigenous peoples of the world, and often that trouble arrived in the name of Christianity. The same dualistic divide also helped to create hierarchical patterns of leadership that most churches still accommodate today; but among Native Americans, for example, in most of their traditional forms, there is no need for such hierarchies.

This western church system included an understanding of orthodoxy over orthopraxis, an understanding that supported the idea that knowledge of a particular subject qualified one as an expert — regardless of experi-

9. Edward Farley, in his attempts to understand the theology and philosophy of Friedrich Schleiermacher, identified the "The Fourfold Pattern of Theological Development" that relegated Christian theology to the areas of: Disciplines of the Bible (text), Church history (history), Systematic theology (truth), and Practical theology (application). See David J. Bosch, *Transforming Mission: Paradigm Shifts in Theology of Mission* (Maryknoll, N.Y.: Orbis Books, 1991), 489-90.

10. Bosch, *Transforming Mission,* 489.

ence. The educational process reinforced the preeminence of the individual over the community. All these notions were contrary to most Native American cultures. Indigenous models tend not to categorize theology as a subject, but even when they do, it's generally recognized that all theology is done in, for, and by the local community, and that it is always the elders or wisdom keepers who are the only ones considered to be the experts. Similarities to indigenous ways of thinking can be found in some strands of pre-Enlightenment European theology, especially in Eastern Orthodoxy.

Theology and worldviews affected by dualism, in this context, moved in a historical line from ancient Greek philosophers such as Plato and Aristotle, to European philosophers such as Descartes and Francis Bacon. These influences eventually led to the particular American dualism that I will address later in this chapter. But first, how do we view the effects of dualism without wading too deeply into the complex mire of philosophy? In many ways, it may be easier to see the Enlightenment as embodied by a particular cultural renewal movement.

Empire Building Finds a Home in America

The European Enlightenment was preceded by and paralleled the European Renaissance. The Renaissance was a return to the cultural and intellectual forms of the ancient Greeks. European art, literature, architecture, and such were all influenced by the "classical" era of the Greeks, and sometimes of the Roman Empire. During the Renaissance, empire in its classical forms was glamorized and utilized in new ways. The cultural Renaissance worked well as a vehicle to transport the philosophical and democratic ideas of the Greeks and the military prowess of the Romans, in order to make empire building seem both romantic and right. These influences also found a home in America. For example, one need only look at the early architecture in the United States capital, Washington, D.C., to see the influence of ancient Greek civilization on America's founders and on the generations that followed them.

Holding on to the culture of the Renaissance on one arm and the philosophy of the Enlightenment on the other, Europeans, and later Americans, were ready to expand their particular brand of culture through conquest to the rest of the world. These influences enabled them to first romanticize, and later to theologically and philosophically justify, their exploits while they devastated the presumed "uncivilized" indigenous peoples throughout the rest of the world. The unfortunate philosophical re-sults from European ideas of civilization were that societies around the world were now bound in dualism. Globally, these colonized nations sprouted an array of common values including materialism, extreme indi-vidualism, a warped view of progress, moralizing, either/or-ism, the tor-ture of both humans and nature, and the philosophical sense of superiority expressed in nationalistic exceptionalism.

After the Enlightenment, reason would come to trump both nature and experience; modern science would posit a false split between the "verifi-able objective" and the subjective experience; causality would come to reign over purpose; the so-called "primitive state" would always give way to "pro-gressively advanced" civilizations; all problems would be seen as solvable; everything would become knowable; and the individual would rise over the communal to possess autonomous authority. In this new paradigm, it was inevitable that the mystery surrounding God would disappear, and even when God was credited, human intellect would reign supreme.

Within such a worldview all creation was expected to serve the pur-poses of the nations who wielded Euro-western thinking. Those nations who were less "enlightened" were expected to accept their destiny, namely to serve the "enlightened nations" through their enslavement and the ex-ploitation of their resources. In Europe, and in America, dualism found a secure home. Even Jesus Christ, the shalom of God, was expected to bow to European theologies of conquest. I am reminded of the simple verse in Scripture that reads, "But don't just listen to God's word. You must do what it says. Otherwise, you are only fooling yourselves" (James 1:22 NLT). After the Enlightenment, the ruse was complete.

Being and Doing

Among Native Americans we don't talk much about God. Strangely, though, I have met only a few Native American atheists or agnostics in my entire life. It is commonly assumed among Native Americans that people's actions will show their understanding of the Creator. Naturally, most Native Americans would not talk much about their theological "belief system" be-cause we don't view our beliefs as separate from simply living out our lives. I have, however, heard indigenous elders talk about their beliefs as they per-tain to a Harmony Way worldview, while mentioning specific values. They might say, for example, "My belief is to be honest" or "to have courage" or "to follow the harmony way of life." In this sense, Native American values and practice could be deemed what some might label as "beliefs." The structure of the conversation among Euro-Americans is very different.

Among Euro-American Christians it is common for a person to understand their faith in terms of their theological beliefs. Whether stating a theological position like "I'm a Calvinist," or taking a denominational stance like "I believe in holiness," or even saying "I subscribe to the doctrinal statement of the National Association of Evangelicals," Euro-American Christians have a firm *idea* that there exists a connection between what they believe and how they live. Unfortunately, European and American history is replete with ungodly people doing god-awful things, including land theft, rape, murder, enslavement, torture, pollution, depleting the earth's resources, and even attempted genocide, by those who held "correct" theological beliefs. There exists a philosophical disconnect in the Euro-western mind between what one believes and what one does. Theologically the disconnect can sometimes be unnerving, but it is usually resolved through the written word.

European and American cultures highly prize the written word. Questions are easily solved in these cultures by seeking the written answer. Whether it is in the Bible, the written law, the constitution, or a particular church Statement of Faith, the answer lies in the written word because they consider the written word the highest form of civilized thinking. Euro-western civilizations always ask, "What does the law say?" "What does the constitution say?" "What does the Bible say?" These propositional concerns are everyday topics for many Euro-Americans. The written word is given permission to override the heart and conscience of people on almost every occasion.

In the appendix at the end of this chapter I have tried to demonstrate a model of how I understand the religious connection among Native Americans, and how it relates to the religious disconnection of Euro-Americans.

I suggest that when viewing life (religion, education, etc.) through a shalom lens, we can see more clearly the biblical values that God put in place among indigenous peoples, long before America, the present nations of Europe, and even ancient Greece were ever formed. On the other hand, the western worldview, while not all bad, needs to be stripped of all its dualistic formulations. Hopefully, this process, once begun, can move us toward a more praxis- and shalom-oriented worldview. Hopefully, Christians' beliefs will one day be seen more in what they do, not just in what they say.

APPENDIX

Native American and Modern Euro-American Religious Reality

Figure 1: Native American Religious Belief

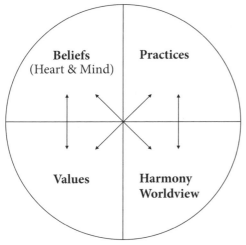

- Beliefs are based on both heart and mind

- Beliefs are consistent with and related to worldview, values, and practices

- The heart, which speaks closely of values (intuition, feelings, sixth sense), should always be trusted

Figure 2: Modern Euro-American Religious Belief

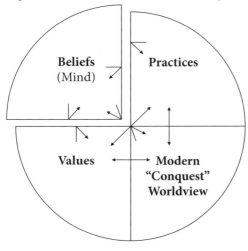

- Beliefs are based primarily on mind (logic, facts, reason)

- Beliefs are separate and inconsistent with, and unrelated to, worldview, values, and practices

- The heart should not be trusted

Figure 3: Native American Religious Reality

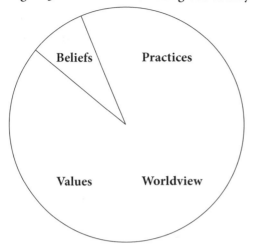

- All of life is religion
- Beliefs are de-emphasized
- Religion is passed on primarily via observation and participation (praxis)
- Correct practices show beliefs and reaffirm values and worldview
- Knowledge is what one has experienced

Figure 4: Euro-American Religious Reality

- Religion is part of life
- Beliefs are over-emphasized
- Religion is passed on primarily via correct doctrine (orthodoxy)
- Correct doctrine shows beliefs
- Knowledge is learned information (facts)

Native American Religious Reality

- Epistemological Orthopraxis
- Truth comes by understanding how others have lived and by living. Mainly taught through story and example. Through this understanding we learn how we are to live. Truth is intimately related to experience.

- Words have primordial power when spoken. The spirit of verbal story is "doctrine" or truth as ceremony, tradition, et al. Explanation weakens the power and makes the words seem less true. Writing words also makes them lose power.
- Circular worldview of harmony/balance seeks to reconcile via integration, accommodation, negotiation. Allows for BOTH/AND options as a primary solution.
- In Christianity this tension is sometimes expressed via concepts like "I am being saved." Ceremony and story over doctrine.
- An example of Harmony worldview might lead to a value of respect, a belief in equality and a practice of mutuality expressed through shared leadership.

Modern Euro-American Religious Reality

- Epistemological Orthodoxy
- Truth comes by learning what others have believed, and comes mainly through doctrine, law, et al. By learning these things one understands how to live. Truth may be unrelated to experience.
- Words have power when written. Spoken word means little. Written word is "doctrine" or truth. Story is for illustration. Explanation, illustration, et al. make words more true and strengthen power.
- Linear worldview of conquest seeks to resolve through conflict via over taking opponent through words, physical aggression and winning/losing strategies. Creates EITHER/OR options as a primary solution. Law of non-contradiction.
- In Christianity this can be seen via concepts like "you are either saved or lost"; "heaven or hell." This worldview values correct doctrine over everything else.
- An example of a conquest worldview might lead to a value of superiority and a practice of racism, classism, sexism, etc. even though the stated belief is equality. In leadership the practice might be expressed through hierarchical leadership.

Characteristics Expressed in Euro-American and Native American Theology and Practice

Native American Theology and Practice

- Creation-Based Theological Foundation
- Harmony/Balance
- Seeks Cooperation with Creation
- Fundamentally Holistic (Shalom)
- Common Spirituality
- Specific Spirituality
- Theology of Place
- Narrative Theology
- Ceremonially Centered
- Local Theology
- Local Polity Expressed in Various Forms of Mutuality
- Present-Centered Christology
- Creator-Son Theological Concept
- Relational Trinity
- Participatory
- Leading to Reflection and Action

Euro-American Theology and Practice

- Redemption-Based Theological Foundation
- Modern "Conquest"
- Seeks to Rule Over Nature
- Fundamentally Fragmentary
- Common Spirituality
- Specific Spirituality
- Theology of Time
- Propositional Truth
- Bible Centered
- Limited Local Theology
- Local Polity Expressed in Various Forms of Hierarchy
- Past- and Future-Centered Christology
- Creator-Father Theological Concept
- Positional Trinity
- Non-Participatory
- Leading to Reflection and Affirmation

CHAPTER SIX

When Time and Place Collide

Past Nothing

It was characteristically dry on a warm July day near Salem, Oregon. The powwow, although it started late, was actually right on schedule since it was running on "Indian time." Just after the Grand Entry ceremonies, one could take a good whiff of the air and notice there still lingered in the air the sweet smell of burning white sage used by the drum-singers and the dancers who had blessed themselves with it earlier. The announcer, in typical emcee fashion as at almost any powwow, was making jokes during the transition time between Grand Entry and the first set of regular dances.

"How many white people do we have here today with us?" the emcee asked the crowd. "Great!" "We want to give you a welcome gift today." "You'll probably want to come up to the announcer's booth sometime soon and get your free Indian pills." With perfect timing he paused, grabbing the attention of every non-Indian present. He continued, "These pills work fast! Within 30 minutes you'll notice a definite lack of craving money, land, and power." The crowd burst into laughter while nervous, half-embarrassed, half-perplexed white folks began to laugh along with everyone else.

Periodic jokes at the expense of the dominant white society continue throughout the powwow, like, "We are still accepting reparations for our stolen land, so don't forget to visit the casino on your way out tonight." Strangely, everyone realizes this joking is done in the spirit of welcome and fun, while at the same time, on another, deeper level, at least to some degree, the truth of the situation stings everyone present.

Having watched the expressions on the faces of white visitors during such times and having even held conversations around the topic, I admit that I have mixed feelings about the jokes. On such occasions there is the initial shock factor occurring among the white people. I think most white people think the issue of stolen land is a *fait accompli,* but for many Native Americans the issue of land will continue to be unsettled until justice is finally served. Does this mean Native Americans live in the past? Not really, because the injustices caused by these issues continue to this very day. On the other hand, there does tend to be a difference in time orientation between Native American cultures and the dominant culture.

Past, Present, and Future Time Orientation

North American Native people today have been influenced severely by modernity, including the influences of our cultural orientations to time. Yet, at events such as powwows and other social and traditional functions, and even at many Native churches (which tend to be bastions of assimilation), "Indian time" often remains the standard.

In the fall of 2007 I surveyed 100 Canadian and American Indians concerning, among other things, time orientation.[1] The results showed that 65/100 of those surveyed agreed that their understanding of the Native American Harmony Way included a time orientation that emphasized the Past and Present. In North America, modern concepts of time constraints influence almost everyone who participates in the dominant culture. Because my survey was done online, it naturally leads to the conclusion that many of those who responded have been strongly influenced by the modern time orientation of the dominant culture (meaning they have online access, can negotiate an online survey, etc.). Given that context, 65 percent can easily be interpreted to mean our Native American understanding of time is still a strong influence, even today.

Time orientation can be a difficult concept to visualize. When people

1. Randy Woodley, *"The Harmony Way"*: *Integrating Indigenous Values within Native North American Theology and Mission* (Ph.D. dissertation, Asbury Theological Seminary, 2010).

run their lives according to a clock, it is easy to segment time into concrete meaning. For instance, at 8:30 a.m. work expectations begin, at noon we may expect to eat lunch, etcetera. It is more difficult to talk about time orientation when viewed as an abstract reality.

In a well-known but admittedly dated study, often referred to in academia as *The Values Project,* time-orientation categories were developed by anthropologists Florence R. Kluckhohn and Fred L. Strodtbeck.[2] The study is still valuable today for my purposes because it included two Native American cultures that at the time were still somewhat unaffected by modernity. The Values Project considered past, present, and future orientations among five people groups.[3] Included in the study were two distinctly different Native American populations, both of which were found to be primarily Past and Present oriented, as opposed to the dominant white cultures, which were found to be Present and Future oriented. Kluckhohn and Strodtbeck summarized the Native time orientation best by stating that a past and present time orientation is "a source of knowledge and continuity that keeps the Present stable and the Future predictable"[4] and that "time was not viewed as a commodity."[5]

In modern western cultures, time is viewed and used as a commodity in order to propel us toward the future, or somehow move us ahead in life. In the dominant American culture we believe we can "make time," "take time," "save time," and "find time," as if time were an actual commodity. Our modern reality is segmented into scheduling our days, hours, and minutes on our calendars. Without the guide of scheduled time, many of us would be lost. Although Present and Future time orientation has be-

2. This study is dated anthropology, written at a time when indigenous/emic categories were just coming to the fore, but Kluckhohn and Strodtbeck are still heavily invested in social science categories. It is necessary to deconstruct and reconstruct their work to get at Native concepts and values.

3. Past, meaning they focus on the time before now and upon maintaining and preserving traditional teachings and beliefs. Present, meaning they focus upon what is now and upon accommodating changes in traditions and beliefs. Future, meaning they focus upon the time to come and planning ahead or seeking new ways to replace the old.

4. Clyde Kluckhohn, Florence Rockwood, and Fred L. Strodtbeck, *Variations in Value Orientations* (Evanston, Ill.: Row, Peterson, 1961), 325.

5. Kluckhohn, Rockwood, and Strodtbeck, *Value Orientations,* 331. In my research I also found scholars in other fields ascribing this same value to Native Americans, i.e., "an orientation to the past which honors tradition, and to the present in taking life as it comes" (Kelley) and "Orientation to the present. Being, rather than becoming" (Evergreen). See Woodley, dissertation.

come a central motif in the dominant American culture, it does not need to remain fixed. Nonindigenous social scientists have been suggesting for decades that there is something the modern west can learn from indigenous societies, including an interest in the relationship that indigenous peoples have to time and how it affects shalom living.

Non-Native Bridges

At this point it occurs to me that readers from the dominant Euro-American white culture may be looking for a little relief from the sting of my views. If this is the case, there is some good news at hand! The research of several non-Native American religious scholars who have tried to understand other indigenous worldviews and well-being concepts has aided Present- and Future-oriented thinkers in imagining other ways a society can relate to time orientation. For example, Joachim Wach's idea of a "cosmic order" reveals that much about the Creator and the creation cannot be reduced to mere words and concepts. Wach felt that people who were bound to an imposed modern time could move beyond the imposed cognitive realm and learn to experience the Creator in every sense, including the emotive, the physical, and the intuitive realms.[6]

A part of the realm of experiences and feelings is the concept described by scholar of comparative religions Rudolf Otto as *Mysterium Tremendum*,[7] meaning that thinking about God includes an element of "awefulness,"[8] "overpoweringness" or majesty,[9] and "urgency"[10] uniquely associated with the divine being. Otto describes this *a priori* sense as a deep reverence felt toward the deity. Otto's thoughts appear to align with the Native American idea of the deity as the "Great Mystery," which in part means that we have much more to wonder about the deity than we are able to know. This type of understanding can move western thinkers back to a more primal sense of time.

Mircea Eliade is another scholar who may shed light from a western

6. Joachim Wach, *Sociology of Religion* (Chicago: University of Chicago Press, 1970).

7. Rudolf Otto, *The Idea of the Holy: An Inquiry into the Non-rational Factor in the Idea of the Divine and Its Relation to the Rational* (New York: Oxford University Press, 1963), 12.

8. Otto, *Idea of the Holy*, 13.

9. Otto, *Idea of the Holy*, 19.

10. Otto, *Idea of the Holy*, 23.

perspective on the many facets of Native American spirituality in his discussion of concepts such as the cosmogonic value of ritual,[11] *imago mundi,*[12] and *homo religiosus.*[13] I think Eliade would understand our Native American rituals as bringing order into the world out of chaos, for we do, in a sense, re-create the sacredness of creation in our ceremonies and we are *a priori* religious beings.

In attempting to understand God and human response to the concept of God, Euro-western researchers and others have, sometimes even without realizing it, built bridges of mutual understanding between the worlds of modernity and more indigenous views of time. By wanting to understand humans at a basic primal level, Euro-westerners can find much to relate to among indigenous peoples. After all, all peoples were indigenous at some point in history.

Same Time and Place — Different Realities

As referenced earlier, in 1917, venerated Keetoowah Medicine Man Redbird Smith spoke of his understanding of religion and the present by saying, "This religion does not teach me to concern myself of the life that shall be after this, but it does teach me to be concerned with what my everyday life should be."[14] In Smith's view, the present is where his spirituality exists. His worldview seems to have little concern for the future. The value of past and present cosmic orientation can be reduced to a micro-level to help us understand how Native American life is perceived on a daily basis. For instance, I have heard Native Americans say of people who operate within the confines of the dominant culture, "they have a clock inside their head," meaning, they live their life in relation to a tighter time schedule than do Indians. In order to understand the natural rhythm of traditional Indians, especially those living in traditional communities on reservations, one's tightly bound time schedule must become less rigid.

My friend Ray Aldred told me a story about a new missionary on an

---

11. Mircea Eliade, *The Sacred and the Profane: The Nature of Religion* (New York: Harcourt, 1987), 12.

12. Eliade, *The Sacred and the Profane,* 43.

13. Eliade, *The Sacred and the Profane,* 44.

14. William A. Young, *Quest for Harmony: Native American Spiritual Traditions* (Indianapolis: Hackett, 2002), 149.

Indian reservation. It seems he wanted to get to know the people better, so he was driving around one of the neighborhoods. He suddenly pulled over when he saw what appeared to be a strange sight. As he got closer he was able to verify his initial impression. It was an elder standing out in front of his house, holding a goat in his arms. Every so often the goat would stretch his neck out and take a bite of the bushes in the elder's yard. The missionary approached the man and asked him what he was doing. The elder replied, "I'm trimming my hedges." This seemed absurd to the young missionary. So he thought about it, and then said, "Don't you know that could take all day?" The old man looked at the missionary with sympathetic eyes as he replied, "What's time to a goat?"

Sometimes conflicts arise when Native Americans adjust poorly to the dominant culture's value of time. In some ways we live in two different realities. While it may seem like a good use of time to people from western cultures to mark the hours and even the minutes, Native Americans lean more toward valuing the organic interactions of place and people. The idea of *place* is also related to creation-based spirituality. The Kantian philosophical divide concerning the concepts of *time* and *space* was ideally a balance of western and nonwestern thought. Yet, the west historically ended up placing the emphasis on *time*. The western time emphasis depreciated serious thinking concerning *space* (or what I prefer to call *place*). When thinking about a creation-based spirituality, *place* takes on relational aspects that are often neglected by an emphasis on time.

Time lends itself to being event-oriented. I understand modern Americans to have adopted a sort of temporal materialism that lends itself toward marking events and neglecting actual concerns about place. The importance of these events becomes a *pseudo-place* from which they draw their identity. For example, Americans everywhere in the world are known for wanting to celebrate the Fourth of July and Thanksgiving, regardless of their global location.

It also appears to me that event-oriented people can adapt easily to changes in locale. New generations of event-oriented people are able to pass down the myth of *pseudo-place,* whereas land-based, place-oriented peoples seem to be more bound to a *real place* and understand it as a basis for their identity. When place-oriented people are removed from meaningful place, such as when Native Americans were removed from their homelands, they have great difficulty adjusting. Often, such differing views of time mean that people end up talking right past each other, as noted in the following quote.

When the domestic ideology is divided according to American Indian and Western European immigrant, however, the fundamental difference is one of great philosophical importance. American Indians hold their lands — place — as having the highest possible meaning, and all their statements are made with this reference point in mind. . . . When one group [American Indian] is concerned with the philosophical problem of space and the other [western European immigrant] with the philosophical problem of time, the statements of either group do not make much sense when transferred from one context to the other without proper consideration of what is happening.[15]

The two different understandings concerning time are important if we are to understand "Indian time" as a value that goes far beyond just "being late." Vine Deloria Jr. believed that place-oriented peoples are concerned with truth in their own context, whereas time-oriented people tend to make truth abstract and apply it to any situation at any time. People who hold truth to be abstract may tend toward having grandiose feelings of superiority since they believe they hold the truth that everyone else should believe. Says Vine Deloria Jr.,

American Indians and other tribal peoples did not take this path in interpreting revelations and religious experiences. The structure of their religious traditions is taken directly from the world around them, from their relationships with other forms of life. Context is therefore all-important for both practice and the understanding of reality. The places where revelations were experienced were remembered and set aside as locations where, through rituals and ceremonials, the people could once again communicate with the spirits. Thousands of years of occupancy on their lands taught tribal peoples the sacred landscapes for which they were responsible and gradually the structure of ceremonial reality became clear. It was not what people believed to be true that was important but what they experienced as true. Hence revelation was seen as a continuous process of adjustment to the natural surroundings and not as a specific message valid for all times and places.[16]

15. Vine Deloria Jr. and Daniel R. Wildcat, *Power and Place: Indian Education in America* (Golden, Colo.: Fulcrum, 2001), 143.

16. Vine Deloria Jr., *God Is Red: An Indian View of Religion* (Golden, Colo.: Fulcrum, 2003), 65-66.

A temporal worldview has limitations since it must have a real beginning and a real end. For instance, the western mind is much more concerned about whether or not a story is factual. Indigenous peoples generally look at story for the truth in it and try to understand how it can be applied. Place-oriented worldviews have no need to project this extreme view of historic and future reality upon themselves or others. With Native Americans, the value of the now is the critical moment. The future has not happened. Again, this is easily illustrated by American Indian ideas concerning "Indian time." What "Indian time" means practically is that our events and appointments will begin when everyone eventually shows up, despite any plans to have folks there at a certain time reflected by the clock. Indian time is regulated by place, relationship, and the experience of the now, not by a clock.

Future Determined by Looking to the Past

Native Americans depend upon our stories, ceremonies, and traditions to guide us to a good future. Often indigenous views of the future are best expressed through exploring experiences from the past. In a sense, we mine our past and those gems become our payment to the future. That is why our stories and other past concerns are so very important. Without our past, we cannot be a people of the future. My *Mi'kmaq* friend Terry LeBlanc tells the story of his grandfather taking him deep into the woods when he was younger. His grandfather told him to look twice as much at the scenery behind him as he moved forward, because if he did not recognize where he had been, he would never find his way out of those woods. This story has become a metaphor for Terry as he speaks on this subject.

I have noticed that when sharing their thoughts, Native American elders often drift freely between current and past events. They may begin a story by saying it began a long time ago, but it is most likely that the behavior or problem they wish to address is occurring in the present. Among Native American values is the understanding that authority is earned through reflected experience. We learn about how to live now, through examining what has happened in our history, especially through the eyes of our elders.

For many Native Americans, even those influenced by modernity, it is by viewing the importance of the past that we receive instructions enough to be critical in the way we live the present. Only after considering the past can we project what our future might be. It is not as though Native Americans don't consider the future, but I suggest that there is an ethos understood among Native Americans that all things will eventually unfold in their own time. As I understand it, this is not a casuistic statement but rather one that reveals the primacy of living in the moment.

In the same way that there is a relationship between Native American views of the past and the present, there is a relationship between the present and the future. It has been said that what we do today will impact the next seven generations. This is a widely held warning among Native Americans when considering the relationship of our present decisions and how they will affect those in the future. Among North American Native peoples, our past is forever in the present, especially when it comes to place.

Theological Place and Placement

Place-based thinking is a foreign concept to most settler peoples. Those who have immigrated to America relatively recently (within the past five hundred years) relate to the world more in terms of a linear time orientation as opposed to a place. The west lacks a theology of place, particularly as it relates to the indigenous (Host People) and immigrant people's context. Certainly, the ancient Hebrew people thought similarly to other indigenes, and the Scriptures are replete with their references to place. Earthly images taken from the Genesis accounts of the garden of Eden are stories of real earth and real earthbound creation.

In the Scriptures, these earthly places set the context for the life of all creation as it is intended to be, that is, in fellowship with the Creator. In Genesis chapter 2 the story is clear that the specific place called "Eden" had a divine purpose: namely, it was the context for all creation to dwell together in shalom with their Creator. Beyond the garden of Eden are the stories of many other physical places, each with a similar purpose of discovering God in a particular place and learning how to best live in a sacred way on that particular land. The background of stories like the garden of Eden, journeys beyond Babel, and Abraham's journey probably informed much of the rabbi Paul's understanding of "the nations" or *ethnē* when he said, "His purpose was for the nations to seek after God and perhaps feel their way toward him and find him — though he is not far from any one of us" (Acts 17:27 NLT).

In the same speech Paul said, "From one man he created all the nations throughout the whole earth. He decided beforehand when they should rise and fall, and he determined their boundaries" (Acts 17:26, NLT). The divine purpose found in verse 27 and in the theology of journey most often means that a particular land, at least for a season, is meant for a particular *ethnē* (people from a particular ethnic group). Regardless of one's view of determination and free will, the Scriptures indicate that land, all land, is attached to divine purpose and that certain lands are meant to host a particular people at certain times.

One with the Land

As a particular land with "boundaries" (Acts 17:27) becomes inhabited, that group of people with a common language and common physical characteristics form a common gene pool, a common diet, a common lifestyle, etcetera. The group becomes uniquely shaped by the land as the land becomes uniquely shaped by them.

Indigenous people of a particular land become "married" to the land, being forever shaped by that land, even if they are later dispersed. Isaiah uses marriage language where he says, "Thou shalt no more be termed Forsaken; neither shall thy land any more be termed Desolate: but thou shalt be called Hephzibah, and thy land Beulah: for the LORD delighteth in thee, and thy land shall be married" (Isa. 62:3-5 KJV). Isaiah's words reveal a clear image of people at home with their land, even married ("Beulah") to the land. How do people become married to the land?

As a metaphor the concept of a marriage can explain the deep love and devotion that any people may have for their land, but marriage is more intimate than mere contact. The Scripture speaks of those being married as "becoming one." Indigenous peoples understand themselves as inseparable from the land. Indigenous peoples know their land. They recognize every hill, spring, and tree. Indigenous peoples know how the land responds to the weather and the seasons.

Lands set aside for particular ethnic groups are like a family photo album from which people can recall what happened to whom and where it happened. The land records the memories. There are sacred places in such lands — places of covenant with Creator, places of healings and miracles, places where ceremonies and traditions take place. For indigenous peoples, the land is home and words like "mother earth" come close to expressing the intimate connection they have to their land. The speech of Chief Seattle expresses this kind of intimacy.

> Every part of this soil is sacred in the estimation of my people. Every hillside, every valley, every plain and grove, has been hallowed by some sad or happy event in days long vanished. Even the rocks, which seem to be dumb and dead as they swelter in the sun along the silent shore, thrill with memories of stirring events connected with the lives of my people, and the very dust upon which you now stand responds more lovingly to their footsteps than yours, because it is rich with the blood of our ancestors, and our bare feet are conscious of the sympathetic touch.[17]

Research from biologist Dr. Thomas E. Reimchen shows that repeated contact between creatures in the same environment literally leaves a trail. Dr. Reimchen studies the interaction between bears and spawning salmon. The bears carry large numbers of dead or dying salmon into the woods for feasting, and in the process may be responsible for relocating important nutrients from the streams into the forests. Reimchen's research has found stable nitrogen isotopes in the tree rings that are historical indicators of marine-derived nutrient transfers into coastal forests. Says Reimchen,

> The salmon in effect are actually feeding the forest, contributing a vital nutrient that it would otherwise not possess. It turns out that of all the nitrogen found in the trees in these watershed areas, commonly over 100 metres from the river's edge, 30 to 40 percent comes directly from these salmon carcasses or from different species that have utilized the salmon and have cycled the nutrients into the vegetation directly or indirectly. In areas where the salmon are found in high numbers (sometimes up to 100,000 salmon per two kilometres of river) up to 80 to 85 percent of all of the nitrogen in these giant trees in fact is derived from salmon carcasses. . . . There is no separation between these ecosystems. These areas exist as part of a continuum; they cannot be

17. Authentic text of Chief Seattle's Treaty Oration — 1854 [Originally published in the *Seattle Sunday Star,* October 29, 1887]. For a discussion of the controversy surrounding Chief Seattle's words, see *The Truth of Chief Seattle* by Joyce E. Meredith and William C. Steele, http://www.pantheist.net/society/truth_of_chief_seattle.html, last accessed on May 31, 2011.

dealt with as separate units because the nutrients cycling the flow of energy between them [are] part of this continuous process.[18]

Dr. Reimchen's research opens up the supposition that in some very real ways people may also be a part of the land itself, and vice versa. If such real elemental transfers do occur in other parts of creation, it would make it difficult for any creature to be thought of as isolated from the rest of creation. Instead of treating humans as separate from the land, we should realize that there are vital connections that are made among all creatures sharing the earth. In the end, it is quite inescapable that we all return to the dirt and become a part of the earth's cycles once again.

Abraham

The defense of a promised land in the Hebrew Scriptures as a result of the Abrahamic covenant is evident, even sometimes overstated,[19] but according to the same Bible, God has a similar concern, not just for Israel, but for all lands. As mentioned earlier, in Amos 9:7 (NLT) God, apparently speaking to the ancient Hebrews, asks, "Do you Israelites think you are more important to me than the Ethiopians? I brought you out of Egypt, but have I not done as much for other nations, too? I brought the Philistines from Crete and led the Arameans out of Kir." The question is rhetorical, but I feel I must restate it in order to break through the popular narrative. God is making the case that Israel should realize they are no more important than any other nation! In fact, God is saying that he has a similar covenant relationship with many, perhaps even *all* other nations! Notice that God even includes his relationship with the Philistines in this brief sampling.

Traditional Native American narratives describe how the Creator's covenant has been extended to our tribes, nations, or people groups and has existed for thousands of years. Many of our Native North American nations, perhaps all of them, have, or at least may have once had, stories about their particular covenant with the Creator. It may be helpful to ex-

---

18. http://www.sacredbalance.com/web/drilldown.html?sku=43, last accessed on May 31, 2011.

19. The Joshua narrative of bloodthirsty terrorists killing men, women, and children is one such overstatement from a Jewish nationalistic redaction.

plore the dynamics of the place-purpose theology I am referring to by sharing one of the many stories. I will share the story of our ancient Keetoowah (Cherokee) people.[20]

Divine Covenant among America's Indigenes

The people who would eventually become the ethnic group whom most of America knows as "Cherokees" (more properly referred to as "Keetoowah") once wandered from their ancient island home. They traveled north and north again, meaning they were a long time heading north. Finally, they began heading east, and eventually their journey led them to the Ohio Valley. At this time the people, for whatever reasons, separated and each of the Iroquois tribes were formed.

Some of the people went northeast and become the Huron or Wyandotte; some of the people went north and became the Onondaga, Mohawk, Oneida, Cayuga, and Seneca; some of the people went west and became the Erie (later the Mingo), the Wenro, and other tribes; some of the people went east and became the Susquehannock. Those who went to the southeast became the Nottoway, the Tuscarora, and possibly others. Those who became Keetoowah people went due south until a sign was given for the seven clan leaders to go upon a particular mountain to fast and pray for seven nights. During this time they saw snow, rain, lightning, hail, and a rainbow. On the final day a messenger from the Creator appeared.

The messenger told them that he was sent by the Creator to tell them that the land they were presently in was the land the Creator had chosen for them since the world began. The messenger explained to them their boundaries and the ways they were to take care of the land. He also told

---

20. By sharing this story I am not violating any tribal codes. See Georgia Rae Leeds, *The United Keetoowah Band of Cherokee Indians in Oklahoma* (New York: Peter Lang, 1996), and Howard L. Meredith, Virginia E. Milan, and Wesley Proctor, *A Cherokee Vision of Eloh'* (Muskogee, Okla.: Indian University Press, Bacone College, 1981). I should note that my story is a compilation of several versions of the same story as told by various Keetoowah people, and this version and its subsequent conclusions will have twists and nuances unique to my own understanding. However, the basic commonalities of all the versions of the story are the same. It is also important to note that there are many accounts of Keetoowah origins; each may have one piece of the whole picture. Cherokee origins are hotly debated among the archeological community, so I acknowledge that I am not attempting to claim a new theory or dispute an existing one. I am simply stating a version of our ancient myth. Undoubtedly, some of the other Iroquois nations will have very different accounts of their role in our story.

them how to live in the Harmony Way with one another and with others who were not their people. He said the Creator's name was *"Yo-wah"* and their name was *"Keet-yo-wah,"* meaning to be "covered or protected under the Creator."[21] The Keetoowah covenant land boundaries included parts of modern-day North Carolina, Virginia, West Virginia, South Carolina, Kentucky, Tennessee, Georgia, and Alabama.

The Keetoowah connection to the land is reinforced through the stories of the land, the ceremonies, traditions, and such. Within these are references to particular places, plants, and animals that are all found in Cherokee country. Our very identity is embedded in the land and through our relationship with the Creator.

The Keetoowah story is just one story among hundreds of those heard among North America's indigenes. Other indigenous people around the world have similar stories, to be sure. Perhaps these covenant stories may help colonial settler peoples to understand more of the meaning of land to aboriginal peoples, especially those who have been removed from their homelands. Resistance to these removals was not just about inconvenience or fondness for the land; it tore away at the very core identity of the people being removed. Removing indigenous peoples from their lands forced them to abandon their sacred covenants with the Creator, causing a tremendous loss of core identity.

Defiled Land

According to Scripture land can be blessed, cursed, defiled, and redeemed. The issue of land is central throughout the Bible, whether it is the garden, the promised land, the Hebrews marking places with piles of rocks, the exiles, the return to the promised land, the Jerusalem cult, or the New Jerusalem. Almost all events in Scripture take place on the land. Land is sacred in God's eyes. God takes these sacred boundaries so seriously that land theft is considered on the same level with idolatry, incest, and injustice toward widows, orphans, and strangers. An example of this is found in the context of the following Scripture passage: "Cursed is anyone who moves their neighbor's boundary stone" (Deut. 27:17a NLT).

Land theft in Scripture, in and of itself, seems not only to bring a curse upon the people of the land, but the land itself can be spiritually de-

21. Per Dave Whitekiller in Leeds, *Keetoowah,* 1996.

filed or polluted. I have found that among indigenous peoples there are many who believe that the land can become spiritually defiled as a result of people's activities. Perhaps this defilement is even a cause for God replacing one people group with another.[22] Leviticus 18:24-30 states,

> Do not defile yourselves in any of these ways, for the people I am driving out before you have defiled themselves in all these ways. Because the entire land has become defiled, I am punishing the people who live there. I will cause the land to vomit them out. You must obey all my decrees and regulations. You must not commit any of these detestable sins. This applies both to native-born Israelites and to the foreigners living among you. All these detestable activities are practiced by the people of the land where I am taking you, and this is how the land has become defiled. So do not defile the land and give it a reason to vomit you out, as it will vomit out the people who live there now. Whoever commits any of these detestable sins will be cut off from the community of Israel. So obey my instructions, and do not defile yourselves by committing any of these detestable practices that were committed by the people who lived in the land before you. I am the LORD your God.

While some people might dismiss the interpretation of land defilement to be simply a part of the priestly code, we should note that there seems to be agreement from both the priestly and prophetic traditions concerning the subject. For instance, the priest Ezra mentions the past warnings from the prophets by stating, "Your servants the prophets warned us when they said, 'The land you are entering to possess is totally defiled by the detestable practices of the people living there. From one end to the other, the land is filled with corruption'" (Ezra 9:11 NLT). In Leviticus 18 the land "vomits" the people from it. What kinds of corruption can people commit that would cause the land to "vomit" them out?

Besides the sexual sins of immorality mentioned in Leviticus 18, others from both the prophetic and priestly traditions include disobedience, covenant breaking (broken treaties), wickedness, bloodshed, and idolatry (see Isa. 24:1-6, and including divorce, as in Jer. 3:1; Num. 35:33; Jer. 16:18; and 2 Sam. 21). Notice how these passages reveal a direct connection between the people's actions and the way the earth responds: "The earth

---

22. For example, perhaps God allows the land to deal with people according to their own transgressions and they are removed through weather anomalies.

dries up and withers" (Isa. 24:4). Because of people's wickedness all creation is affected, including flora, fauna, and wildlife: "How long will the land lie parched and the grass in every field be withered? Because those who live in it are wicked, the animals and birds have perished" (Jer. 12:4).

Similar to the references in ancient Israel attributing the corruption of the land to evil committed on the land are other indigenous accounts throughout history. For example, James Adair, a member of the Irish gentry who lived among the Southeastern tribes, noted the presumed relationship between sexual immorality and judgment during the smallpox epidemic suffered by the Cherokee in 1738. The Cherokees, he said, believed that the disease was punishment for the increase in adultery among the young people.[23]

In Job chapter 31, Job defends his own righteousness by mentioning his care for orphans, taking care of the poor, lack of trust in money, and hospitality to strangers. In making his own defense to God, Job calls to witness both his own servants and the land itself. "If my land accuses me and all its furrows cry out together, or if I have stolen its crops or murdered its owners, then let thistles grow on that land instead of wheat, and weeds instead of barley" (Job 31:38-40 NLT). If the land can be cursed for misuse, it appears it can also be blessed for the proper use for which it was intended.

In his book *Healing the Land: A Supernatural View of Ecology*, Maori author Winkie Pratney points out the ecological judgments and blessings that appear to correspond with people's actions. According to Pratney, "When we abandon our posts as God's good stewards of any area of the Kingdom of God, including territory that formerly welcomed God, we block His needed hand of protection."[24] Pratney continues to point out a similar view in Ezekiel chapter 14, which includes judgments of famine (v. 13), ecological devastation (v. 15), war (v. 17), and disease (vv. 19-20). There certainly appears to be no shortage of blocking God's hand from blessing America in our materialistic, consumer-driven, wasteful society.

Americans tend to be pragmatic people except when they are held captive to a false ideology. I wonder what it will take for us to hear the sound of the alarm going off in our world right now. I will leave it to the dozens of other books out there to explain the specifics of our impending disaster and

---

23. Samuel Cole Williams, *Adair's History of the American Indians* (Johnson City, Tenn.: Watauga, 1930), 244-45.

24. Winkie Pratney, *Healing the Land: A Supernatural View of Ecology* (Grand Rapids: Chosen Books, 1993), 142.

only note that topsoil is disappearing . . . forests are shrinking . . . desertification is advancing . . . coral reefs are dying . . . plants, fish, insects, birds, and animal species are all going extinct . . . and our freshwater sources are being depleted! Serious concerns exist at every level from local to global.

For millennia, the whole of creation has been producing enough energy to allow limited consumption. Humanity, in just a few generations, has accelerated consumption exponentially. Mother Earth is now trying to rebalance the overuse through random "acts of nature." She is reclaiming her territory, "spitting out the inhabitants," in order to restore harmony. As each new season brings increased natural disasters on us such as floods, violent storms, acid rain, and serious global water shortages, it appears that we have blocked the Creator's blessing in some significant ways.

Looking at the problem from a global perspective, the normal energy supplied by Mother Earth through producers such as phytoplankton are being consumed too rapidly and disequilibrium has occurred. Under normal conditions (i.e., premodern), humans are only tertiary consumers of the earth's energy, behind more primary consumers like zooplankton and secondary consumers like fish. Humans have moved recently from tertiary consumers to becoming primary consumers. Such change is beyond the earth's natural cycles and recharge rates, creating imbalance and disharmony on the whole planet. In order to restore balance, the earth is being forced to "consume" the primary consumer, moving her temporarily to confront humanity with the only defense she has, namely, natural disasters. In a very real sense, the top of the food chain is now the earth herself. But hopefully, there may still be time to repent and change.

"The blessings for an obedient nation are much more numerous than the judgments,"[25] observes Pratney. He references Leviticus 26 for a list of the blessings on the land, including ecological health (v. 4), economic health (v. 5), personal security (v. 6a), civil security (v. 6b), international security (vv. 7-8a), honor and growth (v. 9), innovation and creativity (v. 10), and God's habitation, not just visitation (vv. 11-12).[26] When all of these blessings are combined we may begin to recognize the description as a familiar reminder of God's shalom intentions for all humanity. We can easily make the connection between our actions when we keep or break shalom, and how our actions affect the earth, including all the creatures that inhabit the earth.

25. Pratney, *Healing the Land*, 142.
26. Pratney, *Healing the Land*, 142.

The blessings of a healed land seem to follow when there is a remarriage between the people and the land. The current marital status between modern humanity and the land is similar to a state of divorce. Today, the earth is clearly speaking to humanity, but in terms of our national and global policies we are ignoring her message. What is needed in order to reconcile the marriage is a marriage counselor. And that is the role that indigenous people can play in this serious breach. Before colonialism eventually eliminates the most precious gift that indigenous people have to offer the world, which is their view of the land, nonindigenous people (those who currently wield the power) need the opportunity to change their worldview and save the planet. It is time for the younger brothers and sisters on the land to learn from their elder brothers and sisters, just how to fall in love with the land once again. If we cannot reconcile this marriage, the effects may be irreversible and it may be sooner than we think.

The apostle Paul captures the intimacy of the relationship between the people and the land when he says, "For we know that all creation has been groaning as in the pains of childbirth right up to the present time" (Rom. 8:22 NLT). Earlier, Paul described the same expectation, using the same language for humans. The point is, both human beings together with all the rest of creation await a better way of living than they may be experiencing now. Certainly, we are already behind schedule.

Righteous Land Use

There are some important prescriptive narratives in the Bible that point to the righteous ways land can be used by both immigrants and host peoples. Using the biblical narrative of Abraham and the Canaanites, Norman C. Habel contends that the host people of the land have an inherent right to "own, share, sell, and negotiate the use of the land in the host country."[27] He explains further:

> The immigrant ideology of the Abraham narratives has a totally different perspective on land entitlement in relation to the Canaanites. The locus of political power lies with the Canaanite people who share their land with the immigrant family of Abraham. They are the host peo-

27. Norman C. Habel, *The Land Is Mine: Six Biblical Land Ideologies* (Minneapolis: Fortress Press, 1995), 132.

ples, and Canaan is the host country. In none of Abraham's dealings with these people is their right to possess the land in question. Nor are they, as a totality, regularly depicted as enemies or unbelievers who deserve to be expunged from the land. Abraham even tries to rescue the sinful Sodomites and pays a tithe to the priest-king of Salem. Abraham respects the Canaanites, their culture, their god, and their territories. Where land is in dispute he negotiates peaceful settlements. When the land is attacked, he fights for the people of the land. When he needs a burial site for Sarah, he buys land in accordance with the local laws of land purchase. Abraham is a peaceful immigrant who willingly recognizes the entitlements of the peoples of the host country. Even the promise to Abraham about future possession of the land focuses on Abraham mediating blessings to other families of the land, rather than on the annihilation of his hosts. In these narratives the peoples of the land are blessed through contact with Abraham. Melchizedek, in turn, calls down the blessing of *El Elyon,* the god of Salem, upon Abraham. Thus Abraham, the head of the first ancestral household and family, becomes a model of responsible power in peaceful negotiations and legal acquisitions of land.[28]

I have come to think of the Abraham migration story as a meta-narrative for all host and immigrant peoples because it is consistent with the hospitality culture of the day, with a christological hermeneutic, and with shalom. The narrative shows that the true authority of the land, without question, rests within the hands of the host people of the land. Again, I point out that the apostle Paul affirms the sovereignty of original host nation status by stating that, concerning all nations, God "determined their boundaries" (Acts 17:26 NLT). Abraham, in his ancient near eastern customs, was simply respecting the national and spiritual boundaries of the Canaanites.

Abraham's journey demonstrates similar values held among many indigenous peoples, including Native North Americans. Traditionally, many tribes teach that when we go into another tribal land, we should first stop at the border and pray, asking permission of the Creator. As soon as possible, a person from the host tribe is sought out in order to give permission, or even a blessing, to those traveling across their boundaries. Even in today's private and impersonal world, these traditions are still practiced

28. Habel, *The Land Is Mine,* 132-33.

among Native Americans. For example, among the great northwest coastal nations we have annual canoe races that have been practiced from time immemorial. A different tribal nation hosts the event each year. Before permanently landing, each canoe must stop at the host tribe's shore and ask permission to come into the host tribe's territory. The host tribe then ceremonially welcomes the visiting tribes to come and enter into their land.

I have had several memorable experiences concerning boundary protocols during the four years our family traveled itinerantly across the United States and Canada. On one such occasion Edith and I were to be plenary speakers at a conference in Phoenix, Arizona. In a dream, just one day prior to our arrival, I was given the message that the host tribe of the land where the conference was to be had not been contacted for permission. Through a series of mishaps, the door to receiving proper permission was closed. Edith and I would not speak in their territory without their permission, so we set about to simply bring gifts to about a dozen tribal elders at the Senior Center of the host tribe and then wait in faith for a possible reconciliation.

As my family and I delivered a dozen traditional gift baskets to the Senior Center, one of the elders asked us who we were. I responded by stating our business in the city and our embarrassment that proper protocol was not sought earlier. I then asked for their forgiveness. I said, "At this point we have no right to ask for your permission but simply want to give you, the host people of the land, gifts for allowing us to visit your territory." I also assured them that we would not be speaking at the conference since we had no permission. I mentioned the fact that we knew there were thousands of deeds to land in that city but that, in the Creator's eyes, they are the ones whom God chose to be responsible for the land. The elders then asked us to stay for lunch.

After getting to know one another for a while, the eldest woman present rose and said a blessing over us and over our conference. She also told us that since we had respected them in this way, the next time we are to speak in the Phoenix area, we need not ask for permission again to be in their land, only "please," she said, "when visiting again, you should come and join us for a meal."

To many Americans, the above illustration must sound incredible. After all, in the average American's mind, they struggled through the current social and economic systems and paid hard-earned money for their homes and their lands, "fair and square." Unfortunately, "fair and square" has a different meaning to the people who were illegally removed from the land for the benefit of Euro-American settlers. In most cases, the land that America's homes, churches, businesses, and parks sit upon today, was stolen from the host people who were here for hundreds and often thousands of years prior to their Euro-American ancestors' arrival.

Waking Up from the American Dream

The historical metanarrative of the *American Dream,* which is accompanied by notions of equality for all, has been used to smooth over historically inconvenient truths and awkward facts of tragedy that have befallen America's indigenous peoples at the willing hands of America's settler population. Americans' wholesale belief in the American Dream makes it difficult for us to face the truth. The truth is, the country that most Americans hold so dear is mostly stolen property. Part of the purpose of the American Dream's familiar narrative is to create a "pseudo-place." The pseudo-place of social location is held in place of real land. The social location acts as a placeholder for real land. In turn, the placeholder of social location deeply influences an American theology of the land.

The American Dream is actually a false premise based on the success of relatively few people, held up as a carrot for the masses. In truth, an American Dream based on the misery of others caters to a selfish, consumer-driven mentality that values wealth and personal gain over justice and peace. The result of such a ruse means that the United States, while originally composed of many Christian individuals, in and outside of its government, was never built on Christian morality. In truth, America is a far cry from being a "Christian nation" or even a nation built upon Christian principles.

Some American Christian historians will concede to this point but qualify it by making a distinction between the original Jamestown and Plymouth settlements. They cite the latter as particularly focused on godly ideals. But we should remember that all three original colonies — Jamestown, Plymouth, and Massachusetts Bay — assumed by proof in their founding charters that the land they sought already belonged to the English king, regardless of whether or not it was already occupied by Native tribes. Whatever the colonialists' Christian goals, they all began their work by asserting their fundamental superiority over the Native inhabitants of North America. In this way, the very foundation of America and the

American Dream was built on a mentality of theft, imperialism, and supposed superiority.

The American Dream continues today to support an American myth of progress via an overarching strand of thought that claims America, while perhaps prone to mistakes in earlier years, has somehow self-corrected by "allowing" civil rights for women and minorities. This belief is simply "whitewashing" the truth by rewriting history from a dominant perspective. The American myth of progress skims over injustices that most Americans would severely critique if they were perpetrated by any other nation, that is, any nation outside the historic Euro-western colonial mentality.

In his book about a similar situation in Australia, *Following Jesus in Invaded Space,* Christopher Budden posits the possibility that one's social location is the primary determinant of one's theology. Budden makes the point that unless Christians are willing to divest themselves of the wrong social location and its associated power, they cannot hope to create an honest theology of the land. Since they have formulated a faulty theology of the land, it must be corrected and an alternative theological narrative must be constructed. Speaking of Australia, Budden states:

> The church, the major holder of ultimate narrative, could find no place for the religious and social claims of Indigenous people. There was little sense that this was a people made in the image of God who could not then be made into the image of white people. There was no sense that this people may have been put on this land by God, or that this people already had some sense of God. There was none of the respect needed to treat Indigenous people as real neighbors, as the "other" whom the church needed to serve justly.[29]

The author draws his conclusions from the life of Jesus, expositing several New Testament texts that reinforce his ideas concerning social location, and then he delves into the way the European invasion has been fitted into their social construction of reality, resulting in a worldview that makes land theft seem as if it is normal. Budden defines racism theoretically and also in the particular context of Australia, which includes *white privilege* and *white normalcy,* two concepts well understood in critical race

---

29. Christopher Budden, *Following Jesus in Invaded Space: Doing Theology on Aboriginal Land* (Eugene, Ore.: Pickwick, 2009), 33.

theory. He also suggests that the way forward is both structural and relational, requiring theological thought concerning the critical question, where is God's presence and location found in a reconstructed theological narrative?

Like Australia, America has created a theological narrative based on freedom, equality, opportunity, and fairness. The imagined values even spin a narrative that props up an idea that America is the place where the divine story uniquely comes together and unfolds as divine providence. Together, these serve as a social location of the American Dream. The false narrative has become in a sense a real place, but the place is amorphous. Instead of *a particular land,* we think of it more in terms as *the* land. America, according to the national myth, is the place of freedom, equality, opportunity, and fairness — not in any one place but "from sea to shining sea." The American Dream inherently contains an ethic of extreme competition, even to the point where we believe we must fight others (read "kill others") in order to be free and in order to retain our divinely bestowed values.

Unfortunately, this false narrative of the American Dream has not brought us the promises of God found in shalom. Instead, the American Dream has supported classism, racism, sexism, and the exploitation of the poor and marginalized, in this country and in other nations. Perhaps above all else, in order to maintain our "Dream" we have incorporated an ethic of war.

Warmongers

Americans have been at war (meaning wars in which American citizens or colonists were engaged) since they first entered the continent as European settlers. In the early days they say the Indians thought it strange how the Europeans, who were at war with one another in Europe, came all the way across the ocean to build forts just to fight against each other here, on this continent. We do well to remember these wars in honor of those who died, including both military and civilian casualties.

At the time of this writing Americans are engaged in three wars, including the invasion of Afghanistan in 2001, the invasion of Iraq in 2003, and the Libyan conflict in 2011. In the decade of the 1990s, Americans fought in Bosnia and Herzegovina and in the Persian Gulf. The 1980s saw the American invasion of Grenada and Panama. In the 1960s and '70s there was the Bay of Pigs invasion and, of course, Vietnam. In the 1950s Americans fought in Korea. The decades of the 1930s and '40s saw us involved in World War II. The decade of the 1920s (and most of the 1930s) was the first decade in over a century that America actually enjoyed an absence of conflict — but remember, just prior to this calm (maybe not so calm when we consider the domestic war on organized crime), was the storm they called the First World War from 1914 to 1918.

Looking at America's involvement in the nineteenth century, in the 1890s was the Spanish American War. The 1860s saw the Civil War. In the 1840s was the Mexican-American War. The War of Texas Independence was fought in the 1830s. The War Against the Creek Indians, the Barbary War, and the War of 1812 were fought in the second decade of the nineteenth century, with Barbary War involvement in the earliest years of the decade as well.

The Franco-American Naval War was fought from 1798 to 1800. The American Revolution occurred in the 1770s and 1780s. The 1750s and 60s witnessed the Cherokee War and perhaps the most forgotten war — the French and Indian War.[30] In the 1740s American colonists were involved in King George's War. Queen Anne's War was 1702-1713. King William's War spanned the decade of the 1680s and 1690s, and New England's reach for land saw war in the 1670s against the Wampanoag, Narragansett, and Nipmuck Indians, known as King Philip's War.

America is far from being a peaceloving and peacekeeping nation, and yet, in the midst of the worst economic decline since the Great Depression, neither political party will consider serious cuts to the military, which by some estimations is the largest single expenditure in the federal budget.[31] Part of the reason Americans are always in conflict is because we are satisfied with a myth that has created a false sense of shalom. Americans feel we already have the divine sense of purpose and the divine destiny God promises, so instead of looking to God for a true model of harmony, we feed our own sense of false harmony by robbing the poor and marginalized in order to maintain our present model. The model we serve, built on conflict, has not served us well.

With a record like ours, Americans cannot make any honest claim of

---

30. In fact, there were periodic clashes with the Indians from first contact until the 1890s.

31. Past and current military spending may take up 54 percent of the federal budget. See http://www.warresisters.org/pages/piechart.htm, last accessed on May 31, 2011.

exercising justice or freedom. Instead, the words of the ancient Hebrew prophets come to mind: "They offer superficial treatments for my people's mortal wound. They give assurances of peace when there is no peace" (Jer. 6:14 NLT). On the other hand, before the arrival of the Europeans, hundreds of North American Native nations were able to live near one another with much less conflict than the Americans. This was due both to the Harmony Way concept that sought multiple peacemaking and peacekeeping strategies and to the nature of war among Native Americans.

The West — It's All about Time

Place is concrete — time is abstract. Within the American myth of *pseudo-place,* most American identity is formed. Because of the inherent dualism in the American myth, the land can have been stolen through egregious means and the national myth can call the nation free — or even, in some cases, Christian! (Many Native Americans say they call this the land of the free because they never paid for it.) The dualistic American myth of *pseudo-place* is inextricably woven into the fabric of history and passed down from generation to generation. Piling injustice and lies one upon the other ensures that there will be no chance in the land for God's intended way for us all to live in shalom. It is as if they believe they can actually remake themselves in whatever place and time in which they find themselves. By contrast, land-based, place-oriented peoples are bound more to a place as a basis for their identity. New ground-rules for bringing such divergent views together are currently underdeveloped.

Place is primarily a relational concept. When the Creator made our world, he was creating the place for relationship between God and all of creation. From that relational place on the earth comes a model of contextualization. God always gives the good news of the welcoming desire for relationship in a particular place (meaning both a physical place and all its cultural accompaniments). We can more easily share God's story as we contextualize the good news to a regional, local, and cultural place. It is common for indigenous peoples to understand the primary emphasis of God's love in terms of place, and as a result, according to relationship in a particular place. The context of relationality, as it relates to place, already exists in indigenous people's own stories.

What has not been presented clearly to Native Americans is the following Christian storyline: Jesus, as the Creator-Son, brought the good news of the relational aspects of the Trinitarian God to earth by creating a place. Eden was where human beings were placed in order to enjoy the fullest possible sense of place on earth. God's original intention was to allow humans to relate in the parameters of a shalom garden. One could say that the garden culture was the original human culture from which one could come to know God, a God who relates in and through community. This divine community is a model for all human societies, including Native Americans. It is this story to which Native Americans can relate, because it is the same story we already know in our own context and in our own place. Each Native American place of covenant is our "Eden."

Western peoples need to develop a more honest history and a shalom-oriented theology, in practical partnership with the indigenous peoples of the world, to gain a better understanding of place. I suggest that the way forward is both structural and relational, requiring honest historical and theological rethinking and a coming to grips with the following concerns: colonialism and neocolonialism; the way current forms of capitalism resist shalom; the way racism affects our thinking and relationships; the practical implications for living on stolen land; how violence is thought to be needed in order to maintain the present system; what true reconciliation looks like. We need to find ways to share power, and we should seek to understand what justice issues are still unresolved among indigenous and other disempowered peoples.

CHAPTER SEVEN

Narrating Our Lives and Ideas:
The Importance of Story

Missing Story Misses Life

Something terrible has happened in modern American society. In our effort to survive modernity and replace actual place with America *the* place, we have failed to develop real stories. Media and mechanization are part of the problem, but the lion's share of the blame is (as previously discussed) how we build our lifestyles around western concepts of time and place. Story (or narrative) takes people to a different realm and a more relaxed frame of mind (read "Indian time"). Modern Americans seldom make time for story in our lives. We usually relegate story to children, even though science is now discovering that listening to stories has a healing effect on adults, including lowering one's blood pressure.[1]

Many modern people are so alienated from place that the created order seems foreign to them. Time (Euro-western time) and "efficiency" are the values that override everything else in our lives. These two shortsighted values, which are in most cases antithetical to shalom, enforce broad categorical assumptions via snap judgments, quick-fix solutions, and prejudice. Mis-prioritized concerns over time and efficiency tend to force communication to be done through brief propositional points. Modern notions of time have taken over American culture to our detriment.

Even the most common greeting heard today, "How are you?" has

---

1. http://www.huffingtonpost.com/dori-baker/storytelling_b_825128.html, last accessed on May 31, 2011.

come to mean less about showing concern for the other and more about a simple acknowledgment that you see a person, whom you actually want to pass by quickly but still want to make them think you have some concern for them, more than you would have for a stranger. What is actually meant is "I acknowledge your presence." In reality, our common greeting does treat people like strangers.

The Missing Church Story

Christian worship in our culture bears no more alternative values than does mainstream American society. Besides being committed to an amorphous structure during certain times of the week, it matters little to modern Christians where their worship experience is located. There is no sense of place in local church theology. As a result, we acquiesce to the cultural values and end up gathering around the idol of Father Time for worship. In such a hurried pace we have become some of the most hypocritical people on earth. We see the same people, week-in and week-out, year-in and year-out, listening to their prayer requests and socializing during the two to five minutes per week we have to share a few words with each other in the busy church schedule. After years of this ritual, we have become so familiar with each other that we can actually fool ourselves into believing that we are true friends. So, instead, we remain "church friends."

Under these circumstances, how deep could such friendships develop? In such a superficial environment, who could ever really get to know one another? I have heard countless times the same experience of Christians who attended a local church for years, only suddenly to realize, "No one really knows me." Certainly human lives are more complex than a shallow structure like modern church allows.

What often happens to Christians today is that we end up with our "church friends" instead of relationships built upon intimacy and sacrifice, which should be a part of our new reality in Christ. This is, really, just being human to one another. In such a scenario, only if one attends a lot of programs and after many years of attendance will one have a chance of moving past superficial relationships. If one can only attend a few programs per week, with most of that time focused on the event and not the building up of our relationships with one another in Christ, then it will actually take many years to move beyond anything more than superficiality.

People want relationships with one another. They want their relationships in Christ to be real, not superficial.

The modern church is trapped in the dilemma of serving modern time. To rationalize our deficit, we have come to believe that making worship services more spiritual or creating better programs will make our dilemma disappear. Christians have come to believe that our spirituality is based upon our own, programmed efforts. This often means that we create a tightly controlled environment (not at all organic like the Spirit), while at the same time sacrificing true community. Several Scripture passages address the problem through a lens of shalom community, going beyond a modern programmed emphasis.

> Then Peter began to speak up. "We've given up everything to follow you," he said. "Yes," Jesus replied, "and I assure you that everyone who has given up house or brothers or sisters or mother or father or children or property, for my sake and for the Good News, will receive now in return a hundred times as many houses, brothers, sisters, mothers, children, and property — along with persecution. And in the world to come that person will have eternal life. But many who are the greatest now will be least important then, and those who seem least important now will be the greatest then." (Mark 10:28-31 NLT)

How do we receive a hundredfold mothers, fathers, brothers, sisters, homes, and children in this life? Surely, not simply by attending Christian-oriented events inside a church building. Shalom community is much more intimate than what is offered at the church building. We do not live the bulk of our lives in the church building, but rather, we live outside the church building, in our homes, at our jobs, and at other places and events. In order to maintain modern American church values, focused around modern notions of time, it is necessary to ignore many biblical passages and toss out a theology of shalom. Passages such as the one below are not meant to fit the cult of Father Time. Fellowship, as expressed in Scripture, cannot be practiced within the confines of the current modern system.

> Above all, love each other deeply, because love covers over a multitude of sins. Offer hospitality to one another without grumbling. Each one should use whatever gift he has received to serve others, faithfully administering God's grace in its various forms. (1 Pet. 4:8-10)

Apparently, in the early church, love happened mostly in homes through hospitality and serving one another with the various giftings that each of us has received. But today, even our theology has had to be adjusted from a narrative, story-based theology, to more precise theologies to fit our culture. In order to accommodate the culture, our preaching must be propositional, our meetings must end by a certain time, and our relationships must be sustained primarily within a rushed time capsule. The tragedy of such a state is that, as followers of Jesus, we do have "the greatest story ever told" but we have forgotten how to tell it!

The Bible is a remarkable book of many stories. It is short on propositional points and long on narrative devices such as imagiNative phrases, symbols, mythos, and backstory. All these stories, in different forms, come together to create a grand narrative of the one Creator designing shalom community for all creation, and becoming a human, in order to show other humans how to live in the shalom community of creation. Found within the story of Christ, our story intersects with God's story and we once again become humans in the way God always intended. As human beings, we all have a story to tell; but when we connect with God in Christ, our story becomes grand but our view of time still determines the story.

Learning to Tell the Story

In a scene from the popular movie *Smoke Signals,* Victor, the young Indian protagonist, is trying to convince his mother that he will keep his word. He asks her if she wants him to sign a paper and she replies, "No way! You know how Indians feel about signing papers!" The fact that Native Americans mistrust the written words in treaties (and well we should) has as much to do with the form of a written document as it does with the content. I have heard elders say "I don't like talking on the phone because I can't see the heart of the person I'm talking to." There is a general mistrust among our Indian people, especially our traditional Indian people, of any form of communication except in a face-to-face encounter. The broken treaties only serve to substantiate the mistrust in all other communicative forms. Referring again to my doctoral dissertation, 75 percent of those Native Americans I surveyed agreed that within their understanding of the Harmony Way there is some sort of primal power in the words of oral tradition.

During my years as a pastor of a Native American church, I encountered the strong belief in story as the primary way people understood the

Bible. If I read from the Scriptures, the more traditionally oriented Indians sometimes politely "tuned out." If I paraphrased the Scriptures in a vernacular more familiar to them, they listened much more attentively. On one particular occasion, some of the more traditional natives in the congregation expressed their thoughts when I asked them about my observations. They said to me, "If we hear it from your heart we will believe you, but we know that the white man translated the Bible and he could have removed things he didn't want us to hear or he could have added things that are not true." Truth, to them, was about hearing the words that come from the heart. From that point on I guess I became a narrative preacher.

By the same token, these same people did not really care for what could be called "expository preaching" (and I still have not located this style in Scripture). They felt that the more good words had to be explained, the less power they had. Given a proper understanding of the Harmony Way, this all makes sense. Our Native American values teach us that each moment is sacred and organic, and when one tries to record those sacred moments outside of the sacred space from which they took place, it could be viewed as presumptuous. Our traditional Indian people tend to feel life should be taken as it comes, with each moment given its due, as it occurs. Canned speeches, propositional reasoning, and expository preaching all tend to move us out of the sacred moment and into a very humanly controlled atmosphere. Somehow, by using shortcuts past the story, and often past the heart, the sacredness of the moment dies.

Even trying to re-create a sacred moment by recording it electronically tends to stifle a mutual sense of trust among some Native Americans. The things that are sacred, we feel, cannot be duplicated well outside of their original context. Using words in a different context from which they were spoken means that the same words can't be judged by the intended community. By that I mean, in Indian country a person must make himself or herself vulnerable in order to be heard. A person's words, along with his or her heart, are judged at that time by the community. If the community that witnessed those words is absent later when they are examined by others, it would be considered out of context. Words taken out of context are not important because they don't impart the same understanding they did when they were given. In other words, words and knowledge, like almost everything else in the Euro-western mind, are a commodity — but they are not to Native Americans.

In Indian country, true knowledge is not so much about facts as it is about gaining an understanding or a revelation from the Creator. I am honored to be a keeper of several traditional items and ceremonies. I was taught by elders, who were keepers of these sacred things, to observe closely when a task was being done and not to ask too many questions. Later, I was given the opportunity to participate and I was corrected when I messed up. I was also told to pray about the things I was learning and to meditate on them. Every so often my questions — which I kept in my heart and mind — would be answered through prayer. As I stated earlier, this learning style was very different from my training in college and seminary, where I was certified based on my knowledge of certain facts that could be verified and transferred to any extraneous context.

Listening Gives Dignity

There is a sacred, historical, and mythical figure, well known among the Dakota, Lakota, and Nakota people, who is sometimes referred to as the White Buffalo Calf Woman. Quoting my Dakota friend, Reverend Fern Cloud,

> Thousands and thousands of years ago White Buffalo Calf Woman brought the pipe to our people and gave us the seven rites along with the seven teachings for us to live by. Through the ways of our people we have to go way back, back to that point in time when everything was in harmony. . . . You hear these themes in our stories and you know if you go to Lakota country, they all have the same ways, sometimes things change a little but basically it's the same.[2]

Here, Fern affirms the oral tradition of her Dakota people, including their ability to endure great periods of time while their stories remain intact. The traditions of our Aboriginal people are not trends or fads. They have been passed down orally for hundreds, thousands, and sometimes tens of thousands of years.[3] Our stories and ceremonies, and the mne-

2. Randy Woodley, *"The Harmony Way": Integrating Indigenous Values within Native North American Theology and Mission* (Ph.D. dissertation, Asbury Theological Seminary, 2010).

3. Our Cherokee Cedar Fire ceremony is an example of a traditional ceremony that traveled with our people before we came to the Smoky Mountains and before we were given our name by the Creator. Even the most conservative estimates would affirm this point in time to be over 10,000 years ago. New forensic science is beginning to point to a 40,000-year point of American entry for Native Americans.

monic objects that accompany these traditions — including places and natural features like the sun, moon, and stars, certain species of animals, trees, and insects — have fairly stable meanings in our stories because of our understanding of their relationship to place. Fern also points to a past Lakota history "when everything was in harmony." The continued passing of oral history also seems to help ensure a return to, or a maintenance of, the Harmony Way.

Adrian Jacobs, a Cayuga, also makes the connection between the power of the Iroquois ancient origins story and their sense of harmony.

> In our Iroquois origin story there is this Tree of Life, which symbolized peace and harmony. Everything works together well and then someone divides the community. In western Christianity it is either/or, and it ends up being cooperation with colonialism and destroys communities. Our story is the codification of human dignity.[4]

Jacobs points out here the original peace and harmony that the Iroquois Confederacy had among themselves until someone "divides the community." He points to the dualism of "either/or" found in western Christianity as something that destroys communities. How do people restore their dignity when it has been lost? According to Jacobs, people restore their dignity by returning to their story, which has been passed down orally from one generation to the next for centuries.

Respectful Communication

When I listen to non-Natives after a cross-cultural encounter with Native Americans, often they use words to describe the affect or manner in which Native Americans communicate, words such as "discreet," "heartfelt," "attentive," "respectful," and "quiet." In my own experiences I know that Indians can get loud, overly expressive, and even boisterous. I state this in order to avoid the danger of stereotyping Native Americans as "stoic." Under many circumstances nothing could be farther from the truth.

With that said, I do believe the observations of my non-Native friends are helpful in pointing out a certain demeanor during more instructive contexts, especially while listening. Because we are primarily an

4. Woodley dissertation, 2010.

oral culture, Native American people tend to exhibit refined listening skills. Indigenous peoples have learned that in order to be attentive, one must be quiet. Listening can be a key to understanding others. If we are listening, we can learn from anyone or anything. Listening is perhaps the greatest compliment one person can pay to another; Adrian Jacobs calls it giving "dignity" to others. "There was a man who crossed the great water in a stone canoe. He brought people to a place of making decisions and listening which dignified listening to one another's stories and it is an affirmation of that dignity to gain consensus among differing views."[5]

Traditionally, First Nations people are taught to listen in all circumstances. For any people who live close to the earth, these skills are vital. When one is hunting, it's not just observations of images that become important but also one's listening skills. For example, a river that is shallow has a bubbling sound, and it is louder than the quiet, sleepy sound of a deep river. A Machupta/Maidu elder once showed me how to listen to the sound of birds while looking for herbal medicines in the woods. The particular sound of the birds, he said, would lead to the medicine being sought. In order to be a culture that values oral tradition and the world around us, Native Americans have learned to be good listeners. Listening is the first lesson of story.

The following Cherokee story of the expansion of the world has many teaching points, but primary among them is that we should listen first to those among us who are the oldest, because their wisdom is based upon much reflected experience. Although I have heard this story told by others, I have a particular fondness for the way Cherokee storyteller Robert Francis relates the story.

> When the earth was first made, it was covered all over with water except for one small island. This island was the top of a high mountain. This was Blue Mountain, in the Cherokee country. White folks came a short time ago and named this mountain Clingman's Dome, no doubt after some white man or other named Clingman. But it has always been Blue Mountain and always will be Blue Mountain. For the Cherokees, the Ani-Kituwa, the Ani-Yvwiya, this is where it begins.
>
> Everyone lived together on this mountaintop island. The human beings and the animals all got along fine. In those days they could understand one another's speech, for this was before the humans broke

5. Woodley dissertation, 2010.

144

the harmony. The animals were also much bigger in those days. In fact, the animals of today are but shadows of those who once were. It was a good place to live. Sure, the island was small, but it was what everyone knew and was used to. All were content, until there came to be more of them than the small bit of land could support.

As they noticed they were getting crowded, a general council of all the people (both humans and animals) was called. The question was asked, "What can we do?" The only answer given was, "We can pray. All we can do is pray and ask the Grandfather Above to please give us some more land."

So all the people prayed, and Creator/Apportioner answered, "Oh my precious children, there is nothing I enjoy so much as giving good gifts to my children. But if I do everything for you without asking you to help in any way, how will you ever learn any responsibility? I really want to teach you some responsibility. Here's what I will do: If one of you will swim to the bottom of the ocean and bring up some mud, just a little bit of mud, I will take that mud, that little bit of mud, and make a whole great land of it."

All the people (animals and humans) began to look at one another. Someone asked, "Who will go? Who will get the mud?" A slow, deep voice answered, "I will go. I will get the mud." It was Grandma Turtle. "Grandma Turtle, you can't go!" they said. "You're too old and slow. We don't know what it's like down there. We don't know how deep it is." "I'll go," quacked Duck. "Now that's more like it," they said. "You're a good swimmer, Duck. You can go; you can do it."

Duck paddled out onto the ocean and dived, but he popped right back up to the surface. Duck dived again and again and again, but the same thing happened each time. Well, you know how ducks are. They dive well, but they float much better. Duck paddled back to shore, shook the water off his tail and said, "I can't dive that deep. I float too well."

The question was asked again, "Who will go? Who will get the mud?" Grandma Turtle said, "I will go. I will get the mud." "Grandma Turtle," they said, "we settled that before! You can't go. You're too old. Who will go? Who will get the mud? Hey Otter, how about you?" "What?" Otter said. "How about you going to get the mud?" "Mud? What mud?" "The mud we need so Creator/Apportioner can make more land!" "Oh, sure," said Otter, and he slid off into the water and was gone a good long while.

When he came back, he had a fish in his mouth, but no mud. Without a word to anyone, Otter climbed up onto the beach and began munching on the fish. Everyone was watching him, but Otter paid them no mind, just kept eating his fish. "Hey Otter!" someone yelled. "What?" Otter said. "Where's the mud?" "Mud? What mud?" Otter asked. "Ohhh the mud! Well, I left here to go and get it. Then I got started playing. Then I caught this fish. Then I forgot all about the ummm, ummmm, whatever it was I was supposed to get."

Oh my! They were nearly at their wits' end. "Who will go?" they all asked. "Who will get the mud?" Grandma Turtle said, "I will go. I will get the mud." No one even paid her any mind. "Who will go? Who will get the mud?" "I will go," said Beaver. "I will get the mud. I don't play, and I do not eat fish."

Resolutely, Beaver swam out into the ocean. He took a deep, deep breath and dived. Wow, Beaver was gone a long time. Some of the people watching and waiting were holding their breath in sympathy, but none seemed able to hold it that long. Finally, Beaver popped to the surface gasping for air. He swam to shore and climbed onto the beach shaking his head. "It's too deep!" Beaver said. "I don't know how deep it is. I never reached the bottom."

Everyone was in despair. Beaver was the last best hope. How would they ever get mud? Maybe there would never be anything but the little mountaintop island. "Who will go?" they asked. "Who will get the mud?" A slow deep voice answered, "I will go. I will get the mud." "You can't go, Grandma Turtle, you're too. . . ." "I WILL GO! I WILL GET THE MUD!"

There were no other volunteers, so they let Grandma Turtle go. She slowly paddled her way out onto the surface of the ocean. As everyone watched, she took a slow, deep breath, then another and another and another. She took three more breaths and disappeared beneath the water. They waited a long time. Grandma Turtle was gone much longer than Duck or Otter or even Beaver had been. She was gone all that day and the next and the next and the next. They posted a sentry up on the very top of the mountain. Finally, on the seventh day, the sentry called out, "I think I see something coming up. Yes, yes, something is rising in the water. Could it be? Could it be? Yes! It's Grandma Turtle!"

Sure enough, Grandma Turtle rose to the surface of the ocean, and there she lay, not moving, with her legs, her tail, her head all hanging down. . . . Grandma Turtle was dead. Quietly, reverently, Duck, Otter, and Beaver swam out and drew Grandma Turtle's body to the shore. They pulled her up on the beach, as all the people (humans and animals) gathered sadly around, and what's this? There, under her front feet, they found . . . mud.

Someone took the mud, that little bit of mud from under Grandma Turtle's front feet, rolled it into a ball and lifted it up toward the sky. The Grandfather took that mud, that little bit of mud and cast it out, making this whole, great land that many nations call Turtle Island.[6]

One of the things that I have learned must be emphasized to those in Euro-American cultures while trying to sensitize them to Native American cultures, is not to interrupt when an elder is speaking. This is one of the cardinal rules in Indian country; but unless they are warned, and even sometimes with a warning, Euro-Americans, to the dismay of the Natives present, will freely start talking right in the middle of an elder's sentence. This behavior exemplifies a huge difference between Native American values concerning elders and the dominant Euro-American cultural values. Among Native Americans, respect for elders goes beyond rules about interruptions. Indians are taught to give the seats to elders first, to assist by carrying things for them or by opening doors, to never send an elder away from a meal without a "to go" plate, and to always bring a gift when visiting an elder. Elders are considered to be the most important members of the Indian community. They are valued and respected *a priori* and for the vital role they play in the community.

Indians who hear the Grandmother Turtle story are not surprised to hear that Grandmother Turtle's actions turn out to be those that save the community. She represents the oldest and wisest of the group. Conversely, they understand that the situation will not improve until the elder is heard and until her suggestions are heeded. As modern Americans begin to try and understand shalom in the community of creation, they should realize that it requires patience and listening to the elders. In this case, the elders are the indigenous peoples who have been living with this land we call "Turtle Island" for thousands of years, especially those elders who represent the Grandmother Turtle.

6. Per Robert Francis, used with permission.

CHAPTER EIGHT

Joining the Party: Essential Community

Doing Shalom

There is a palpable sense of community among most indigenous people groups. Sometimes the Native American community can be viewed as protective and guarding and sometimes it appears to be inviting and expanding. Whether protective or inviting, the sense of group cohesion is apparent to outsiders. How does such an *esprit de corps* form? When one is far from his or her tribe and homeland, the generic term "Native American" takes on new meaning. In urban settings, where Native Americans are usually the smallest of all minority populations, one can observe friendships far beyond tribal lines. Sometimes these friendships are even extended among traditional tribal enemies. Jesus' community of creation calls us to recognize each other, beyond our tribal lines or race, class, gender, and ethnicity and to love our enemies in a likewise fashion.

Similar to Native American family values, the mark of a successfully balanced Christian community is a group of people who pray together, sing together, eat together, and do outreach together as they continue to create a visible community environment. Modern America is a very individualistic society. Followers of Jesus need to challenge the assumptions by which we choose to fellowship. I suggest we need both — new models and older, even ancient models — to help us create a composite of how Christian community may look as it practices shalom in the community of creation.

Native American families, like most indigenous societies that are not too far removed from an age when survival meant depending upon one's family, are traditionally close and each member is valued. In the recent past, how that family and how the individuals within that family conducted themselves could have dire consequences for the whole group. Because of this potential danger, each person had a serious role to assume and the expectations of each role were clear. The same ethos was transferred to the person. Each person was valued to be as important as the other, since it took everyone to sustain the tribe, clan, or family. Diversity was highly valued. Perhaps a way that Native American societies differ from the dominant culture is found in our view of diversity.

The Harmony Way consists of a sense of unity and diversity that recognizes an individual, not just for how they can continue the family's survival, but for their uniqueness and giftedness as an individual person. This is shared in light of a similar ethos found in 1 Corinthians 12:12ff., where Paul states that each part of Christ's body is as important as the other. In the dominant culture, unity and diversity mean something different than in Native American culture.

The difference between these two cultural perceptions is that among most dominant cultures, including white American culture, unity is actually uniformity — which is valued over diversity. When diversity is devalued, the most dominant cultural force becomes the standard for what is normal. That current standard of normal in America is white, upper-middle-class culture. What is sad in American Christianity is that the cultural standard for "Christian" is also white upper-middle-class culture. American evangelical Christians are not particularly known for their ethnic and cultural diversity. In contrast to uniformity, each of us should be viewed as important *because* we are different. We are designed to be different because together, we can manifest the wisdom and beauty of God in a fuller way than we can separately.

Christ's witness on earth is impeded by American Christianity's homogeneous cultural views and by the failure of Christians to appreciate divergent theological and cultural views. Working toward tolerance is a place to begin, but even tolerance is not usually the best solution to a lack of diversity. To tolerate difference is often the same as to ignore it. I believe that today God is calling Christians beyond tolerance and toward celebrating the uniqueness of the other. We should also realize that only after Christians have worked through our own dirty laundry will we have the credibility to affect all the systems in the world that God wants to change. The goal of shalom community is to influence all these systems with shalom. A shalom lifestyle is God's way of dealing with the world and its problems. Shalom is meant to be an alternative model for the rest of the world and to provide an alternative to all the systems in our world that have been corrupted. This is how the hoop gets mended.

In our own Native American story, the Christ of past mission models presented to our people has not been able to mend the broken hoop. The gospel, as it has most often been preached to Native Americans, does not promise us restored balance or harmony. Actually, too often, the gospel preached to Native Americans and other indigenous peoples around the world was quite the contrary to good news. We have mostly heard the gospel as "bad news."

The "bad news" of Jesus Christ requires people to forsake their own ethnic identity for the identity of the dominant culture. The "bad news" of Jesus Christ means trading in shared communal values for economic systems based on greed and the success of the individual over the group. The "bad news" of Jesus Christ requires indigenous peoples to accept their status as those meant to be colonized and to cooperate with their own demise. The "bad news of Jesus Christ" asks us to draw our theology, values, and meaning as people from a culture that wishes to make us self-haters. If Native Americans and other indigenes succumb to "gospel" demands as presented by many of our missionary friends, then we will actually become circle breakers, not circle keepers.

To live out shalom on earth requires a change in the present culture, including and especially among Christians. Shalom must be allowed to take over our decision-making, reform the way we have done things in the past, and inform our future. If we are to make a decision to live out shalom in the world, we must begin by changing our American culture. We must remove the legacy of colonialism, not just forget it, and we must see the connection between theft, injustice, and the abuse of power, including how they help to create poor and oppressed peoples, and how they serve to exploit and destroy the earth.

> There are those who move boundary stones;
> they pasture flocks they have stolen.
> They drive away the orphan's donkey
> and take the widow's ox in pledge.
> They thrust the needy from the path
> and force all the poor of the land into hiding. (Job 24:2-4 NIV)

If we are to rescue our planet, which is currently bent on a trajectory of destruction, then Christians must begin to live out shalom, even by changing their own church cultures. The initial cultural dilemma that presented itself when Native Americans first met the European settlers is the same cultural dilemma we face today, namely, that Native Americans, who do not claim to know Jesus, live life much closer to a shalom-based, biblical Christianity than do the people who claim to be Christians.

What Needs to Change?

Native American spirituality and shalom spirituality are both primarily concerned with maintaining harmony in cooperation with creation, the Creator, and others. The materialistic values of the Euro-American modern culture imposed upon Native Americans is very different than our own indigenous values. Take, for instance, the Protestant work ethic that drives the nation so hard. The Protestant work ethic is foreign to most Indians. Nature always provided our needs in the past. No one worked just for the sake of working. Indians are generally not materialistic, so gathering material wealth was unimportant. The cultural practices that served America's aboriginal peoples so well in the past have a residual effect today and must be negotiated with modernity and its demands.

The stark differences between Native North American values and those of the dominant Euro-American society have been noted throughout our mutual history. How we work, why we work, what we share, what we save, who we share with, how much we share, are all concerns of Jesus and a shalom-based spirituality. The differences between modern Americans and what Jesus taught are also striking. Differences concerning economics reveal the state of our hearts, and our hearts reveal the state of our faith. Concerning wealth and material gain, Jesus said in Matthew 6:24, "No one can serve two masters." Native Americans would tend to agree with Jesus on this matter. Historically, this attitude can be demonstrated. The following quotes demonstrate how one tribe, the Cherokee, understood wealth.

> The problems were those which arise wherever a stable, collective system and one based on expansion and individual profits collide. It was, for instance, impossible to run a store or plantation profitably without violating the way of reciprocity fundamental to most Amerindian so-

cieties. To obtain respect in the Native world, people had to redistribute wealth; for esteem in the white world, they had to hoard it. To a Cherokee, sufficient was enough; to a white, more was everything.[1]

The Cherokee concept of redistribution of wealth is at direct odds with the individualism expressed in modern American values. Until the nineteenth century, the Cherokees were able to retain their communal values, even after suffering the deaths of thousands of their fellow tribal members as a result of removal from their homelands. U.S. Senator Henry Dawes, after touring Indian Territory in 1887, describes the economic state of the Cherokees in Oklahoma.

> The head chief told us that there was not a family in the whole nation that had not a home of its own. There is not a pauper in that nation, and the nation does not owe a dollar. It built its own capital . . . and built its schools and hospitals. Yet the defect of the system was apparent. They have got as far as they can go, because they hold their land in common. . . . There is no selfishness, which is at the bottom of civilization. Till these people will consent to give up their lands, and divide them among their citizens so that each can own the land he cultivates, they will not make much progress.[2]

Progress, according to Senator Dawes, was equated with individualism, materialism, and even selfishness. None of these are Cherokee values, nor do they represent the cultural norms and values of other Native Americans. These norms concerning wealth are still a present cultural clash. The following e-mail concerning the Green Corn Dance was sent to me recently as a reminder by a Cherokee friend who attends the traditional Cherokee Stomp Dance Grounds in North Carolina:

> The Cherokee Ceremonial Festival of the Green Corn Moon (which coincides with when the first, thinnest crescent of the moon appears after the "new" or dark moon) will fall on August 20th this year. Celebration in the southeastern nations traditionally includes a lot of preparation.

---

1. Ronald Wright, *Stolen Continents: Five Hundred Years of Conquest and Resistance in the Americas* (New York: Houghton Mifflin, 1992), 207.

2. Scott L. Malcomson, *One Drop of Blood: American Misadventures of Race* (Darby, Penn.: Diane Publishing Company, 2000), 15.

- Houses are cleaned but so are lives.
- Gifts of your extra or excess are given away.
- If you have more than one of anything — any duplicated item — you would give it away before Green Corn starts, preferably to someone who doesn't have that item.
- Extra food is also shared with those who need it.
- Debts are paid, and those who have grudges seek to end them before Green Corn begins.
- Weddings are planned — and divorces become final — before Green Corn's first day.

It was a time of celebration — so to make room for that, it was preceded by a time of reflection and contemplation. So during these days we find ourselves in the midst of preparing for Green Corn.

- We are to prepare our calendars — clear time off to celebrate it correctly by planning ahead.
- We are to prepare our minds — start choosing to do what is right.
- We are to prepare our hearts — begin shedding ourselves of all that might tempt us to be miserly.
- We are to prepare our bodies — medicine is taken, bad habits dropped.
- We are to prepare our home — so our clan may visit and be welcomed.

It is solemn now — but the feast is coming!

The Green Corn Festival, like many indigenous ceremonies, sounds so much like shalom and Jubilee that it is highly probable that the ancient instructions came from the same source. The emphasis is on not collecting too many material possessions. "Extra," "duplicate," and "excess" things are given away as we shed from ourselves temptations to become "miserly." Along with the material things being shed are sickness, bad feelings, and grudges. Then we take on a general sense of restoration of the Harmony Way in our lives. Sometimes the Cherokees refer to this kind of living as walking the "White Path" — the idea being that when we walk in the Harmony Way in all our traditions we are on a pure road or path.

In such a system it does not make sense to stock up on unneeded food too far ahead, thus depleting natural resources and creating a storage problem. Nor does it make sense to hoard food away from the needs of others. Additionally, if the Creator is seen as the supplier of food, it feels presumptive and ungrateful to take more than one needs. When all of these components are considered in deference to one another, there is harmony and the freedom from worry.

Better to Give Than Receive

"The worst thing that can be said about a Navaho is to say, he acts as if he has no relatives."[3] When I moved to western Oklahoma I had only one uncle and aunt in the state, and they were over two hundred miles away. Libby, the Kiowa woman who would become my adopted mother, had lost a son to cancer the previous year and the Creator had shown her that he would be sending her another son. At thirty-three years old, I became that expected son. I was adopted by her family and later by another Kiowa family, as a son. I was adopted as a nephew by a Kiowa/Comanche couple and as a brother by a Cheyenne man. Years later I adopted an elder brother and recently, after our latest move, I have been adopted as a brother by a Cheyenne-Arapahoe man. The formal adoption process among Native Americans is an extension of a deep and profound sense of hospitality to others. Constant visiting among friends and relatives is a hallmark of Native American communities, and no one ever goes away from a gathering hungry. Complete strangers are often given special honor and gifts at pow-wows and at other social functions. Reverend Fern Cloud asks, "How are strangers treated? One of our seven rites is the making of a relative. We really believe that in our way of *wo' dakota,* no one should ever be alone. Someone would take you into their family and adopt you. But today, after so many times of that generosity being burned, we are not as open as we once were. We need to tap into this again and make others family, kinship, living together and supporting each other."[4]

Fern makes a direct connection between hospitality and generosity in the Dakota Harmony Way. There is an insistence that no one should be alone. Alone, people have no protection. Alone, people have no fellowship. Alone, the tribe or clan does not exist and harmony cannot therefore exist.

3. Clyde Kluckhohn, Florence Rockwood, and Fred L. Strodtbeck, *Variations in Value Orientations* (Evanston, Ill.: Row, Peterson, 1961), 320.

4. Randy Woodley, *"The Harmony Way": Integrating Indigenous Values within Native North American Theology and Mission* (Ph.D. dissertation, Asbury Theological Seminary, 2010).

Hospitality and generosity are the natural economy in the Harmony Way community.

Anthropologist Carl Starkloff notes the historic practice of hospitality among Native Americans:

> On reading the various accounts and monographs by explorers and anthropologists, what strikes one is the almost universal hospitality shown by Indian tribes, especially to their White visitors. It is quite remarkable as described in David Bushnell's writings about explorers and missionaries among the Siouan, Algonquian, and Caddoan tribes west of the Mississippi. . . . There are practically no examples of inhospitality or harsh treatment rendered to Whites. On the contrary, the tribal leaders went out of their way to receive these visitors as special guests. There seems to have been a conviction among the Indians, at least until the middle of the 19th century, that they and the newcomers could share the land equally, even if the land was sometimes thought to be the tribes' sacred inheritance.[5]

Starkloff goes on to say that among Native Americans today, "Generosity . . . is practiced . . . almost to excess."[6] In many places throughout Indian Country, I have observed what to Euro-Americans could be seen as exceptional acts of hospitality and generosity, and yet they are practiced normatively today. Every act needn't be lavish among Native Americans.

I was taught by my adopted Kiowa father that any gift from the heart is a good gift. He also taught me that among the Kiowa, if someone compliments you on a piece of jewelry, a hat, or some other object you value, then it is your obligation to give it to them, without begrudging the act. Gift-giving among Native Americans is an act of the heart, regardless of monetary value. The practice is an exercise in nonmaterialism, and it would be a good one for non-Natives to take up.

It is a cultural norm throughout the United States and Canada for Native Americans to have what we call "Give-aways." Native Americans in the Northwest had a similar construct called a Potlatch. I have observed Give-aways in many places with only slight variations. Basically, a Give-away is a formal public ceremony where an individual or family gives away

---

5. Carl Starkloff, *The People of the Center: American Indian Religion and Christianity* (New York: Seabury Press, 1974), 88.

6. Starkloff, *The People of the Center*, 89.

any number of items to other people. The Give-away items may be expensive or not; they may be personally valuable or not. I have seen horses, saddles, rifles, baskets, blankets, money, and many other gifts given away. They may even include sacred items such as drums or eagle feathers. The gifts may be given to strangers, friends, elders, those in need, and other honored guests, but they are not supposed to be given to one's relatives.

The one thing that all Give-aways have in common is that they are given *by,* and not *to,* the person who is being honored. This makes it opposite the cultural norm of the dominant society. The idea is that it is the privilege of the person being honored to give things away. The honored person shows generosity by sharing his or her honor with others in this way, thereby spreading the honor around. Give-aways are routinely done at certain times in Native American culture, including one's first entry as a dancer into the powwow arena, the making of a chief, when a person is given an Indian name, and other celebratory occasions. My wife and I had a Give-away at our wedding, at the time when we all began dancing at powwows, when I was honored with an eagle feather headdress, and at my ordination into Christian ministry. Although the Give-away is seen as a formalized method of generosity, the spirit of generosity pervades nearly all Native American communities.

Give-aways are always done in public, but there is a place in the Indian community for public ceremony and there is a place for subtle giving, with this characteristic differing from tribe to tribe. I have often seen people give without any recognition, for example, by leaving a gift in my home after they visit. More often I have seen straightforward and unencumbered giving when a person simply extends their hand with a gift and expects nothing except perhaps a handshake back. I have also observed occasions when acts of kindness are done for someone in need, especially for elders, and all the while no one seemed to know who did it. I have observed boxes of food being left on a person's porch, cut wood for the winter, and yards cleaned — all without anyone knowing who expressed the generosity. What all these forms of secret or quiet giving have in common is simple generosity from the heart, without fanfare or expectation.

Friends in Low Places

The following story is found in the fifteenth chapter of the Gospel according to Saint Luke. In order to hear this familiar story closer to the way Jesus may have told it, please read it aloud or, if possible, have someone read it to you.

Now all the tax-collectors and sinners were coming near to listen to him. And the Pharisees and the scribes were grumbling and saying, "This fellow welcomes sinners and eats with them."

So he told them this parable: "Which one of you, having a hundred sheep and losing one of them, does not leave the ninety-nine in the wilderness and go after the one that is lost until he finds it? When he has found it, he lays it on his shoulders and rejoices. And when he comes home, he calls together his friends and neighbors, saying to them, 'Rejoice with me, for I have found my sheep that was lost.' Just so, I tell you, there will be more joy in heaven over one sinner who repents than over ninety-nine righteous people who need no repentance.

"Or what woman having ten silver coins, if she loses one of them, does not light a lamp, sweep the house, and search carefully until she finds it? When she has found it, she calls together her friends and neighbors, saying, 'Rejoice with me, for I have found the coin that I had lost.' Just so, I tell you, there is joy in the presence of the angels of God over one sinner who repents."

Then Jesus said, "There was a man who had two sons. The younger of them said to his father, 'Father, give me the share of the property that will belong to me.' So he divided his property between them. A few days later the younger son gathered all he had and traveled to a distant country, and there he squandered his property in dissolute living. When he had spent everything, a severe famine took place throughout that country, and he began to be in need. So he went and hired himself out to one of the citizens of that country, who sent him to his fields to feed the pigs. He would gladly have filled himself with the pods that the pigs were eating; and no one gave him anything. But when he came to himself he said, 'How many of my father's hired hands have bread enough and to spare, but here I am dying of hunger! I will get up and go to my father, and I will say to him, 'Father, I have sinned against heaven and before you; I am no longer worthy to be called your son; treat me like one of your hired hands.' So he set off and went to his father.

"But while he was still far off, his father saw him and was filled with compassion; he ran and put his arms around him and kissed him. Then the son said to him, 'Father, I have sinned against heaven and before you; I am no longer worthy to be called your son.' But the father said to his slaves, 'Quickly, bring out a robe — the best one — and put it on him; put a ring on his finger and sandals on his feet. And get the fatted calf and kill it, and let us eat and celebrate; for this son of mine was dead and is alive again; he was lost and is found!' And they began to celebrate.

"Now his elder son was in the field; and when he came and approached the house, he heard music and dancing. He called one of the slaves and asked what was going on. He replied, 'Your brother has come, and your father has killed the fatted calf, because he has got him back safe and sound.' Then he became angry and refused to go in. His father came out and began to plead with him. But he answered his father, 'Listen! For all these years I have been working like a slave for you, and I have never disobeyed your command; yet you have never given me even a young goat so that I might celebrate with my friends. But when this son of yours came back, who has devoured your property with prostitutes, you killed the fatted calf for him!' Then the father said to him, 'Son, you are always with me, and all that is mine is yours. But we had to celebrate and rejoice, because this brother of yours was dead and has come to life; he was lost and has been found.'"

Like any good story, social context and historical background are critical to a proper understanding. As we inch our way through the narrative, we need to keep reminding ourselves of the big picture. What is the big picture? Luke tells us at the beginning of the story that the Pharisees and scribes, who represent a good portion of the organized religion in Jesus' day, are not happy with Jesus. They had no problem with Jesus feeding sinners, especially when they were among the poor. Part of the duties of any good Jew was to feed the poor. Righteousness was shown in Israel by taking care of widows, orphans, and strangers. Injunctions to assist the needy had been established by Yahweh since ancient times and were all part of the whole Sabbath and shalom ethic. But two things about Jesus' actions concerned the religious leaders and brought them great consternation.

1. The group Jesus was associating himself with was a mixed crowd that likely included all kinds of sinners along with the tax-gatherers. It was as if Jesus was not concerned with whom he fed or hung out. He did not seem bothered by the fact that he would become ritually unclean just by his association. It was obvious to the Pharisees that the tax-gatherers, who

were often seen as extortionists and as traitors to Israel, didn't deserve any special treatment.

2. The religious leaders were upset with Jesus because he was eating with the sinners. For the Pharisees, it was one thing to feed the poor, but it was quite another to sit down at table with them. What was the difference? Dining with someone in Jesus' day, and even today in many cultures, is more than a small act of hospitality. Part of ancient Semitic peacemaking operated by a code of hospitality, including dining at table with people. Even enemies could make amends as a result of eating a simple meal together. In middle-eastern cultures sitting at table with someone was tantamount to giving them your peace or granting them shalom.[7] Such an act meant you cared for their welfare. The very act of Jesus dining with such people infuriated the Pharisees because they did not view the people with whom Jesus was eating worthy of receiving shalom. To the Pharisees, "sinners" lived outside the realm of the holiness codes and they had no right to assume that they were being received by anyone representing God by proxy, much less by God himself.

As a religious leader, Jesus understood well the concerns of the Pharisees and scribes. This story is one of the most tender expressions in the Gospel accounts of Jesus entreating the Pharisees and scribes to understand God's shalom welcome to all people, everywhere, in terms they understood. Surprisingly, the story (or actually three stories) did not begin with so much tenderness.

In each of the stories Jesus asks the religious leaders to imagine their own place in the story. He begins by asking the question, "Which one of you, having a hundred sheep . . ." Stop. To the Pharisees and scribes, what Jesus just said was like a punch in the nose! What was going through their minds when Jesus asked them to imagine themselves as shepherds? While images of shepherding in the Hebrew Testament lend themselves to pas-

---

7. The background to this ancient custom is likely situated in desert cultures, where a meal shared by a stranger meant prolonging his life for another stretch of time. By feeding the stranger, the host was demonstrating concern for the stranger's welfare. The following quote exemplifies the principle as seen in Arabic culture. "Years ago, in the sands of Arabia, there was no more welcome sight to the weary traveler than a black tent on the horizon. Whether it belonged to a friend, a stranger, or even an enemy, a traveler knew that he could claim from its Bedouin owner three days of hospitality. That was the way of the desert and its fame spread all over the world. The black tent became, for many, a symbol of Arab hospitality." http://www.saudiaramcoworld.com/issue/196603/the.black.tent.htm, last accessed on May 31, 2011.

sages like the good shepherds of Ezekiel 34 or Psalm 23, where God is thought of as a shepherd, or even David, the beloved "shepherd king," in Jesus' day such warm analogies no longer applied. Shepherds were respected in ancient pastoral times, but not by urban leaders in the period of the Roman Empire.[8]

Shepherds were not cultural figures to which the scribes and Pharisees wanted to aspire. To the Pharisees and to their spiritual narratives, shepherds were considered virtual strangers. Jesus, after "drawing first blood" in their minds (in reality Jesus was simply trying to restore an ancient truth), urged them to think about the welfare of one lost sheep out of a hundred. Even if the Pharisees could imagine themselves as shepherds, one wonders if they could wrap their heads around leaving ninety-nine other sheep just for the one. In truth, the Pharisees and scribes were probably considering it appropriate to just let the one sheep remain lost so they would be able to care for the ninety-nine.

Then Jesus told a story of a woman who lost a coin. Certainly the irony was not lost on the Pharisees as Jesus attempted to get them to imagine themselves as a woman, who in their society had very few rights. The ten silver coins were likely her dowry, probably the only possession the woman had. The custom was for women to wear the ten silver coins as a headdress. According to Jewish custom, she was allowed to keep her dowry even after her husband died. Since no other members of her family are mentioned, she was probably a widow.[9]

The Pharisees and scribes would not have enjoyed the first two stories Jesus told. They probably liked the reference to them as shepherds better than the reference Jesus made in trying to get them to think of themselves as women. With that in mind, they would likely care less about a widow who lost one-tenth of her dowry. If Jesus was trying to make the religious leaders uncomfortable, he was succeeding. The Pharisees and scribes were now wondering what other insults would follow.

A firstborn son in ancient Semitic patriarchal cultures was consid-

---

8. "Both rabbinic literature, probably reflecting a Pharisaic understanding, and Roman urban elite sources despised shepherds. Because the Pharisees in Jerusalem mostly belonged to people with some resources, most of them probably shared this perspective regarding shepherds. Throughout the literature of this period shepherds are poorly educated, rough, rural people who do not fit the categories of people respected by educated urban audiences." From an e-mail exchange with New Testament scholar Craig Keener, April 23, 2011.

9. Joachim Jeremias, *Rediscovering the Parables: A Landmark Work in New Testament Interpretation* (New York: Charles Scribner's Sons, 1966), 134.

ered the grand prize! The firstborn son had most of the rights and all the authority after his father died. Upon the father's death, the bulk of the inheritance was given to the firstborn son and the remainder was distributed to any other sons.[10] As Jesus began to craft the story familiar to us as "the prodigal son," the Pharisees and scribes would have been feeling considerable disgust at the actions of the younger son. The younger son's demands were viewed as a curse to the family and especially to the father. His actions were unpardonable, tantamount to wishing his father to die.[11] In the midst of all the Pharisees' disgust, Jesus describes the actions of the kind father.

After hearing the father's reactions, the Pharisees must have thought to themselves, "This father was already too indulgent of his second son because he split his estate when the son demanded it." For the father to be in constant vigil, watching for the son, waiting for the day of his return, was also beyond their belief. Then, the intimacy of the welcome the son received — the father running to him, welcoming him with a ring, the family signet symbolizing his acceptance back into the family; a robe, probably the father's own cloak; and a feast, where the best calf is killed and shared with all the servants, slaves, and even the poor of the community — was beyond the Pharisees' scope of reason. "Still," they must have thought to themselves, "if Rabbi Jesus wants me to imagine myself as the kind father, I can entertain such a notion." Perhaps the Pharisees would begin to understand the big picture of God's graciousness as they imagined themselves as the kind father. But wait, the story is not finished.

Enter the elder brother. He was a stodgy coot. He worked his butt off in the way any good son should. He was "nose to the grindstone" all the way, and he knew that after his father's death it would all be worth it. The elder brother resented the younger brother way beyond the scope of forgiveness. And of course, the irresponsible, thoughtless, self-centered second son didn't deserve forgiveness. He had made himself, by his own willful disobedience and foolishness, a virtual orphan. He no longer had a right to claim his own family or any other family as his own. Certainly, the Pharisees could understand where the elder brother was coming from. And then Jesus posits a moment of tenderness in the story. He situates the good father within earshot of the party. In that party everything is good,

---

10. Cf. Deuteronomy 21:17. The elder son would receive double the portion of all other sons.

11. Jeremias, *Rediscovering the Parables*, 128-29.

161

whole, happy. The lost son is restored; family and extended community —
which would include servants, slaves, and even the local poor — are feasting, and the community is whole once again.

The story concludes with the father entreating the elder brother to
come in with him and join the party. The father asks the reluctant son to
party and rejoice with him because the lost one has been found. Only at the
end of the story did the Pharisees and scribes understand that Jesus did not
situate them in the story as the good father. Jesus was drawing a clear conclusion that the Pharisees and scribes were the elder brother. The father,
who represents Jesus, and by proxy, God, was calling the undeserving lost
ones home. Lost sheep, lost coin, and lost sons are all found once again. The
story of the lost sheep, the lost coin, and the lost sons all conclude with a
party! What is the party? The party is God's shalom community.

In God's shalom community, anyone, no matter how undeserved, is
welcome. The Pharisees and scribes finally "got it." They understood that
those tax-gatherers and sinners about whom they were complaining were
being welcomed by Jesus, because welcome and hospitality is the opening
hallmark to living out God's shalom. And in case they lost sight of the bigger picture, they only needed to think a little harder about the story. Let's
recap the social dynamics of the characters in the story.

Almost at the Party

Jesus described the characters of each story in a way that would have made
the Pharisees wonder about their status and thus wonder about their own
standing with God. For example, the shepherd was a kind of a stranger.
The shepherds of Jesus' day were treated like strangers by the urban elite.
Shepherds, as I mentioned earlier, were not welcome even to testify in their
own legal proceedings. The shepherd was a *stranger.*

The woman in the story is seen as not having a husband. If not a
widow, she would have been living with other family members. The Pharisees could have easily assumed that the woman once had a husband who
had died. The woman was a *widow.*

The prodigal son described in the story was by all means legally cut
off from his family. He had asked for his third of his father's inheritance
prior to his father's death, which was scandalous, as if to say he wished his
father to die. He was, deservingly by his own actions, "orphaned" from his
family. The younger son was an *orphan.*

I don't think it is an accident that Jesus, to get the Pharisees to see the wider implications of shalom and true righteousness, in these three stories chose a stranger, a widow, and an orphan. The Pharisees and scribes understood that true righteousness was to take care of these very people. It may be true that the Pharisees did not understand this dynamic right away. Still, Jesus' stories represented at several levels one of the most serious commands in Judaism, that is, to care for those who had few rights and who were the most oppressed and marginalized peoples in society, those represented throughout the Scriptures by the phrase "strangers, widows, and orphans."

Yahweh's concern for the disempowered did not end in the Hebrew Testament. James 1:27 declares, "Religion that is pure and undefiled before God, the Father, is this: to care for orphans and widows in their distress, and to keep oneself unstained by the world." Jesus is trying to help the Pharisees and scribes, the so-called experts in the Torah, to see the bigger picture. The new kingdom he brings is not really so new, since shalom was God's plan from the beginning. What is new is the new way of seeing things. It was God's plan from the beginning to teach the sons and daughters of Abraham, and all other peoples everywhere, to live out life on this planet in shalom or the Harmony Way. In John 3:17, Jesus says, "Indeed, God did not send the Son into the world to condemn the world, but in order that the world might be saved through him." What is this salvation? True salvation is shalom salvation. When is it appropriated? Today. Shalom living is for today.

New Mercy

In order for Christians to muster enough mercy to accept the ramifications of such a broad salvation, we must be willing to rethink our current exclusivist claims on the gospel. We must, as we consider the implications of the numbers Jesus used in these stories, practice mercy. There is a planned progression of numbers here. First, Jesus presents one of one hundred sheep. Next, he references one of ten coins. And finally, his concern (or the concern he is trying to elicit from the Pharisees) is about one of two sons. Why does this sound familiar? The numeric sequencing resonates with the bargaining sequence in Genesis chapter 18, where Abraham is bargaining with God for righteous persons in Sodom.

Shalom living was God's plan for all nations from the beginning.

163

God makes a nation of Abraham specifically for the purposes of spreading shalom as it is demonstrated by practicing justice and righteousness.

> Then the men set out from there, and they looked towards Sodom; and Abraham went with them to set them on their way. The LORD said, "Shall I hide from Abraham what I am about to do, seeing that Abraham shall become a great and mighty nation, and all the nations of the earth shall be blessed in him? No, for I have chosen him, that he may charge his children and his household after him to keep the way of the Lord by doing righteousness and justice; so that the Lord may bring about for Abraham what he has promised him." (Gen. 18:16-19)

When Abraham sees that God is going to destroy Sodom, he has mercy on Sodom and begins bargaining with the Lord. (Note: this may have been the response God was soliciting from Abraham.) In Genesis 18:23 Abraham asks the question, "Will you indeed sweep away the righteous with the wicked?" At that point his bargaining session with God begins. Abraham first asks God if he will spare the city if he finds fifty righteous people. Then he moves to forty-five, then forty, and so on, all the way to ten. God was willing to withhold Sodom's destruction even if ten righteous persons were found in that city. Jesus' sequence goes quicker — one of a hundred, one of ten, and one of two — but he is asking the same question as Abraham and hoping to solicit the same response. "How many will it take for you to take on the same spirit of mercy that characterizes your God?" Where does the condemnation stop and where does the acceptance of those who don't deserve more begin? The answer was clear to Jesus. Acceptance begins with just one. Each and every one.

Ezekiel 16:49 states, "This was the guilt of your sister Sodom: she and her daughters had pride, excess of food, and prosperous ease, but did not aid the poor and needy." Such greedy living habits were clear violations of the hospitality ethic, sharing equity and such, that are God's expectations of people living out shalom. Again, the backdrop narrative of Sodom concerns inhospitality to strangers and not taking care of the poor and needy. This is the same rebuke Jesus makes to the Pharisees. Jesus' stories are trying to get the Pharisees to think about God's willingness to welcome and not condemn others whom they feel don't deserve acceptance into God's shalom community of creation. Jesus is still trying to get us all to do the same.

The story in Luke 15, and really everything Jesus did and said, speaks to us about a new way of living out shalom in the community of creation. My people, and people the world over, understand it as harmony and balance, although it is spoken of with different words among different peoples. The story, our story, is about a party, a community involving all people and all other parts of creation. The party is demonstrated by carrying out justice and righteousness among our fellow humans and the earth and all her other creatures. The community concerns itself especially with the marginalized and disempowered parts of creation that do not have the voice or the power to speak for themselves. This includes strangers, widows, and orphans. It includes the earth herself, and all of her resources. It includes the remaining indigenous peoples. Shalom in the community of creation — life as God intends it — awaits our embrace.

The Return of Beauty

As it was told to me, many years ago the sun took on the human form of a beautiful woman. She traveled each day across the sky. The Sun's daughter lived in the center of the sky, and daily the sun would stop to visit her. The Cherokee people loved the sunshine and the ability to see all of the beauty Creator had made. As time went on, the sun stayed longer each day, lingering until the visits began to cause a great drought. Things were in a terrible mess! People were having heat strokes. The springs, creeks, and rivers all began to dry up and all the crops died. People and animals alike began to starve. The Harmony Way had been broken.

The Cherokee came together with the animals to discuss their serious concerns about the Sun. After days of discussion they could not agree on an answer, so they decided to go to the Little People for their advice. The Little People told the Cherokees, as difficult as it may be, they must kill the Sun.

The Cherokee discussed it and tried to decide who would carry out this monumental task. They first asked the rattlesnake to kill the Sun for them. Grandfather Rattler agreed he would do it, and he coiled himself up by the door to the Sun's daughter's house. When the daughter opened the door for her mother, the snake struck. The Sun's brightness had blinded him though, and by mistake he struck the daughter and she died.

The Sun could not be consoled. She shrouded herself in the clouds as she mourned her daughter, and eventually she stopped shining altogether. Soon, the rains came. At first the rain was a welcome sight. The Cherokee and all the animals thought their problems were solved and that harmony would once again be restored. But the rains continued day after day until they caused tremendous flooding. Soon, no village or any kind of shelter for even the smallest creature would be safe. The Cherokee sought the Little People once again for their advice. The Little People told the Cherokee that they must travel to the west, the land of the spirits, and bring back the spirit of the Sun's daughter. That was the only way to restore harmony.

Seven of the most courageous and most spiritual warriors, armed only with sacred sourwood stick and eagle feathers, traveled west, to the land of the spirits. When the warriors found the spirit of the Sun's daughter, she said she would not return with them. They tried to convince her to come back to Cherokee country with them, but no matter what they said, she was determined to stay in the land of the spirits.

Finally, one of the warriors got an idea. He struck the spirit seven times with his sacred fan and she collapsed. The warriors put her in a large box to travel back home to Cherokee country. On the way back, the spirit of the Sun's daughter awoke. "I am thirsty," she said, but they ignored her request for water. She yelled from the box again, "I am so hungry," she said, but again the warriors ignored her request. Then suddenly, with a more serious tone in her voice she cried out, "I can't breathe. I am going to die!"

The Cherokee warriors became concerned for her, and they opened the box a tiny bit. The spirit darted out, and in mid-flight became a redbird. With her song the daughter began calling out to her mother. Upon hearing her daughter's song, the Sun pushed back the clouds to see her daughter once again. The Sun was very happy to see her daughter in the beautiful form of a redbird, so she allowed her to remain that way and the earth returned to normal. Now, when we see a redbird, we are always reminded that no matter how out of balance things can become, there always awaits a return to beauty.

Bibliography

Arensberg, Conrad M., and Arthur H. Niehoff. "American Cultural Values." In *Introducing Social Change,* ed. Conrad M. Arensberg and Arthur H. Niehoff. Chicago: Aldine Publishing Co., 1971.

Banai, Edward Benton. *The Mishomis Book: The Voice of the Ojibway.* Hayward, Wisc.: Indian Country Communications, 1988.

Barreiro, Jose, ed. *Thinking in Indian: A John Mohawk Reader.* Golden, Colo.: Fulcrum, 2010.

Bell, Brenda, John Gaventa, and John Peters. *We Make the Road by Walking: Conversations on Education and Social Change with Paulo Freire and Myles Horton.* Philadelphia: Temple University Press, 1990.

Bosch, David J. *Transforming Mission: Paradigm Shifts in Theology of Mission.* Maryknoll, N.Y.: Orbis Books, 1991.

Brett, Mark. *Decolonizing God: The Bible in the Tides of Empire.* Sheffield, U.K.: Phoenix Press, 2008.

Brueggemann, Walter. *Peace: Living Toward a Vision.* St. Louis: Chalice Press, 2001.

Budden, Christopher. *Following Jesus in Invaded Space: Doing Theology on Aboriginal Land.* Eugene, Ore.: Pickwick, 2009.

Deloria, Vine, Jr., and Daniel R. Wildcat. *Power and Place: Indian Education in America.* Golden, Colo.: Fulcrum, 2001.

Deloria, Vine, Jr. *God Is Red: An Indian View of Religion.* Golden, Colo.: Fulcrum, 2003.

Duncan, Barbara R., ed. *Living Stories of the Cherokee.* Chapel Hill: University of North Carolina Press, 1998.

Eliade, Mircea. *The Sacred and the Profane: The Nature of Religion.* New York: Harcourt, 1987.

Bibliography

Habel, Norman C. *The Land Is Mine: Six Biblical Land Ideologies.* Minneapolis: Fortress Press, 1995.

Jeremias, Joachim. *Rediscovering the Parables: A Landmark Work in New Testament Interpretation.* New York: Charles Scribner's Sons, 1966.

Kidwell, Clara Sue, Homer Noley, and George E. Tinker. *A Native American Theology.* Maryknoll, N.Y.: Orbis Books, 2003.

Kinzer, Stephen. *Overthrow: America's Century of Regime Change from Hawaii to Iraq.* New York: Times Books, 2006.

Kluckhohn, Clyde, Florence Rockwood, and Fred L. Strodtbeck. *Variations in Value Orientations.* Evanston, Ill.: Row, Peterson, 1961.

Köehler, Ludwig, Walter Baumgartner, and Johann J. Stamm. *The Hebrew and Aramaic Lexicon of the Old Testament: The New Koehler and Baumgartner in English.* Translated by M. E. Richardson. Leiden: E. J. Brill, 1993-.

Leeds, Georgia Rae. *The United Keetoowah Band of Cherokee Indians in Oklahoma.* New York: Peter Lang, 1996.

Lindbeck, George A. *The Nature of Doctrine: Religion and Theology in a Postliberal Age.* Philadelphia: Westminster, 1984.

Malcomson, Scott L. *One Drop of Blood: American Misadventures of Race.* Darby, Penn.: Diane Publishing Company, 2000.

Mander, Jerry. *In the Absence of the Sacred: The Failure of Technology and the Survival of the Indian Nations.* San Francisco: Sierra Club Books, 1992.

McDonough, Sean M. *Christ as Creator: Origins of a New Testament Doctrine.* Oxford: Oxford University Press, 2009.

McGonigal, Terry. *"If You Only Knew What Would Bring Peace": Shalom Theology as the Biblical Foundation for Diversity.* Unpublished, 2010.

McLaren, Brian D. *A New Kind of Christianity: Ten Questions That Are Transforming the Faith.* New York: HarperOne, 2010.

Memmi, Albert. *Colonization and the Colonized.* Boston: Beacon Press, 1991.

Meredith, Howard L., Virginia E. Milan, and Wesley Proctor. *A Cherokee Vision of Eloh'.* Muskogee, Okla.: Indian University Press, Bacone College, 1981.

Mooney, James. *Myths of the Cherokee.* New York: Dover, 1995. (Originally published by the U.S. Government Printing Office, Washington, D.C., in 1900 as *Nineteenth Annual Report of the Bureau of American Ethnology to the Secretary of the Smithsonian Institute.*)

Otto, Rudolf. *The Idea of the Holy: An Inquiry into the Non-rational Factor in the Idea of the Divine and Its Relation to the Rational.* New York: Oxford University Press, 1963.

Plantinga, Cornelius, Jr. *Not the Way It's Supposed to Be: A Breviary of Sin.* Grand Rapids: Eerdmans, 1995.

Polkinghorne, John. *The Trinity and an Entangled World: Relationality in Physical Science and Theology.* Grand Rapids: Eerdmans, 2010.

Powers, Edward A. *Signs of Shalom*. Philadelphia: Joint Educational Development United Church Press, 1973.

Pratney, Winkie. *Healing the Land: A Supernatural View of Ecology*. Grand Rapids: Chosen Books, 1993.

Smith, Andrea. *Conquest: Sexual Violence and American Indian Genocide*. New York: South End Press, 2005.

Starkloff, Carl. *The People of the Center: American Indian Religion and Christianity*. New York: Seabury Press, 1974.

Strong, James. *Strong's Exhaustive Concordance of the Bible with Greek and Hebrew Dictionaries*. Nashville: Royal Publishers, 1979.

Treat, James. *Native and Christian: Indigenous Voices on Religious Identity in the United States and Canada*. New York: Routledge, 1996.

Wach, Joachim. *Sociology of Religion*. Chicago: University of Chicago Press, 1970.

Wallace, Paul. *The Iroquois Book of Life: The White Roots of Peace*. Santa Fe, N.M.: Clear Light Publishing, 1994.

Weaver, Jace. *That the People Might Live: Native American Literatures and Native American Community*. Oxford: Oxford University Press, 1997.

Whiteman, Darrell. *Melanesians and Missionaries: An Ethnohistorical Study of Social and Religious Change in the Southwest Pacific*. Pasadena, Calif.: William Carey Library, 1983.

Williams, Samuel Cole. *Adair's History of the American Indians*. Johnson City, Tenn.: Watauga, 1930.

Woodley, Randy. *Living in Color: Embracing God's Passion for Ethnic Diversity*. Downers Grove, Ill.: InterVarsity, 2001.

———. *"The Harmony Way": Integrating Indigenous Values within Native North American Theology and Mission*. Ph.D. dissertation, Asbury Theological Seminary, 2010.

Wright, Ronald. *Stolen Continents: Five Hundred Years of Conquest and Resistance in the Americas*. New York: Houghton Mifflin, 1992.

Young, William A. *Quest for Harmony: Native American Spiritual Traditions*. Indianapolis: Hackett, 2002.

Zinn, Howard. *A People's History of the United States: 1492-Present*. New York: HarperCollins, 2003.

Index

Aboriginal Rainbow Elders, 43

Abraham: divine covenant with, 122-23; land use of, 128-29; and mercy, 163-64

Activism, 22-24

Adair, James, 126

Adam: as common ancestor, 84-86; fall of, 67-70

Adoption, 154

Advent, 43-47

Afghanistan, 133

Aldred, Ray, 51, 115-16

America. *See* United States

American dream, 131-33

American Revolution, 134

Amos, 15-16

Animals, 37-38, 46; creation of, 42; and disease, 90; and human beings, 50-51; oppression of, 29, 80; soul of, 94

Ants, 49

Aristotle, 104

Australian Aborigines, 19

Authority: over land, 129; in Native American culture, 118

Bacon, Francis, 104

Balance, 23, 68

Barbary War, 134

Bay of Pigs, 134

Beauty, 165-66

Beliefs: in Native American theology, 105; and religion, 96

Benton, Eddie, 82

Birds, 42. *See also* Animals

Blessings: of God, 97; on land, 127-28; and shalom, 13

Body, 94

Bolivia, 64-65

Bosnia and Herzegovina, 133

Brueggemann, Walter: on shalom, 19-21, 24; on well-being, 22

Budden, Christopher, 132-33

Bureau of Indian Affairs, 79-80

Canaanites, 129

Cannibalism, 91

Canticle of the Sun, 56

Capitalism, 97

Cayuga, 123

Ceremonies, 118, 142-43

Chapman, Tracy, 62

Cherokee: on beauty, 165-66; cementation ceremony of, 23; and covenant with creator, 123-24; and creator-son,

kingdom of God, 32-34, 38-40; and
land use, 129-31; makers of, 22-24;
and mercy, 163-65; ministry of, 25-32,
46-47; as peace, 12-14; practice of,
148-51; and reciprocity, 66; and righ-
teousness, 78-80; and society, 15-17;
universality of, 18-20; and war, 134-
35; and world order, 11-14
Shame, 69
Shenandoah, Leon, 81-82
Shepherds: dignity of, 45-46; and Phari-
sees, 160; status of, 162
Sin: and Harmony Way, 67-70; and
land defilement, 125-28; and shalom,
23
Sinners, 158-62
Sioux Nations, 80-82
Skills, 96-97
Smith, Andrea, 63
Smith, Redbird: on Native American
religion, 115; on religion, 77-78
Smithsonian, 95
Social justice, 15-16
Social safety net, 30
Society, 15-17
Sodom, 163-64
Soney, Dave, 90
Soul, 94
Space, 116
Spanish American War, 134
Spirituality: and mystery, 100; of Native
Americans, 67-70, 74-78; and place,
116; and shalom, 151; and time, 115
Spiritual leaders, 73
Starkloff, Carl, 155
Story: of church, 138-40; and life, 137-
38; in Native American culture, 118;
priority on, 140-42; and Scripture,
140
Strodtbeck, Fred L., 113
Sundance, 88
Susquehannock, 123
Sweat lodges, 99-100

Theft: and American dream, 131-32; of
land, 124-28, 130-31
Theology: and indigenous peoples, 61;
of land, 132-33; of place, 119-20; and
social location, 132
Time: in Euro-western culture, 135-37;
as idol, 138; in Native American cul-
ture, 112-18
Torah. *See* Law
Tradition: in Native American culture,
75-76, 118; oral, 140-42, 142-43
Transformation, 22
Trinity, 25. *See also* Creator; God
Truth, 117-18
Tuscarora, 123

United States: and American dream,
131-33; and colonialism, 104-5; education system in, 97; and Native Americans, 95; shalom in, 23-24; and war,
133-35
Urbanization, 51
Utilitarianism, 53-57
Utopia, 11, 21, 75

Values Project, The, 113
Vietnam, 134

Wach, Joachim, 114
War: and America, 133-35; origins of,
78; and shalom, 11, 12-13
War Against the Creek Indians, 134
War of 1812, 134
War of Texas Independence, 134
Wealth, 13; quest for, 101; and shalom,
15, 151-52; sharing of, 35-36
Well-being, 22
Wells, Spencer, 85
Wenro, 123
Whiteman, Darrell, 73-74
Widows, 15-17, 162
Wilderness, 28
Winthrop, John, 45
Wisdom, 97-98

The Seattle School
2510 Elliott Ave.
Seattle, WA 98121
theseattleschool.edu